THE
PHENOMENON OF
PROPHETIC
PRAYER

SHARON RANDOLPH

WESTBOW
PRESS®
A DIVISION OF THOMAS NELSON
& ZONDERVAN

WestBow Press books may be ordered through booksellers or by contacting:

WestBow Press
A Division of Thomas Nelson & Zondervan
1663 Liberty Drive
Bloomington, IN 47403
www.westbowpress.com
844-714-3454

ISBN: 979-8-3850-1045-5 (sc)
ISBN: 979-8-3850-1046-2 (hc)
ISBN: 979-8-3850-1044-8 (e)

Library of Congress Control Number: 2023920085

Print information available on the last page.

WestBow Press rev. date: 07/05/2024

First and foremost, this book is dedicated to my Lord and Savior, Jesus Christ, for His enormous gift of grace and salvation. He's my Rock, Rescuer, Anchor, Peace, Father, Daddy, and God, who makes being a daddy's girl worthwhile. To my Bestie, the Holy Spirit, who has taught me, raised me, and been a super Helper in my walk. I love and adore you.

To my husband, the great encourager, you always want to see the best in others. You have endured the test of time with me as I have birthed this book. I love you forever. I want to thank my children, who have strengthened my character and faith and who love me unconditionally.

To my family at Advancing Christ's Kingdom Global Ministries, you are the best of the harvest. I absolutely love you. To all those who were leaders in the house and who labored and continually pushed me toward the goal, thank you. God has used every experience and everyone who has passed through my life, making this possible.

CONTENTS

FOREWORD

In a time where there is so much turmoil, chaos, fear & a need for stability and hope, Sharon Randolph has come along with a work on prophetic prayer. These two areas are needed in the Body of Christ like never before; the prophetic so that people can receive the Word of the Lord & prayer so that a greater intimacy with the Lord will come to each individual. This treatise is a must read for those searching to understand world events, their lives & help to find hope & solutions in these challenging times. Prophetic prayer is key! Her desire to bring knowledge & wisdom, as well as, application provides the reader with tools to successfully encounter an authentic relationship with God & others. "The Phenomenon of Prophetic Prayer" is written with a push to ignite our prayer lives. She encourages us, through her life experiences to "stick to it" & not give up or give in easily. Prayer & an invasion of God's spirit in the hearts of people is the only answer in our lives, the nation & the world. I have known Sharon for over 25 years & her heart has always been consumed with God's will & God's ways. She has always been one to repeatedly return to "what does the word say?" Her life reflects her relationship with God in her patience, heart for people & seriousness regarding intimacy with the Lord. This book images her own journey in developing a relationship with the Lord, through trials & a persistent "never turn back" mindset. She has pressed through & urges us to do the same. We, of course, learn greatly from what she shares in these pages. She expounds on the importance of being in the word & prayer daily along with developing an ear to hear & discern what the Holy Spirit is speaking to us. In this way, she instructs us to re-focus & discover our life-calling & destiny. Read this book and discover your "super power" through prophetic prayer. It will truly make you, as Sharon puts it "better, stronger, wiser" & I will add "whole"! --*Dr. Jerry & Sherill Piscopo, Evangel Christian Churches Roseville, MI*

PREFACE

I thought it was over. I wondered if I would lose my job. I enjoyed my job, and I didn't want to join the long line for unemployment. In that vulnerable, fearful, and painful moment, I remembered when I would write letters to God—the once Stranger to that eight-year-old girl.

This was my first time writing as an adult. I sat down, not really knowing what to expect or if He'd meet me, and I wrote, "Dear God, You probably know I work at the bank, and I really like my job. A certain amount of money is missing. They don't know where it is, and I don't either, but I want You to protect my job." I thought, *Wow, God, I really poured my heart out to You in a childlike manner, and You answered me, even when I wasn't living for You.* A year had passed from the time I wrote that letter until I read it again.

Someone asked me, "Why are you writing this book?" And from the depths of my heart, I knew that God wanted me to write it all down: the stories, supernatural experiences, and pain that brought me to my yes. I thought about growing up and how I loved to write. I wrote letters to God even though my family didn't know Him, and He was yet a stranger to me. However, there was something within my heart that encouraged me to write. Starting with simple salutations like, "Dear God," I told Him everything and experienced the greatest freedom. In response to why I was writing this book, I say that it for those who only know Him as a stranger and Christians who struggle in their prayer lives and feel frustrated that their prayers aren't answered. I'm writing for the one who doesn't know how to take prayer to another level and for those who are in pain. I'm also writing it for those looking for a remedy, as I once did, and needing a shift, change, or turnaround in their lives. Last but not the least, I am writing it for the God who healed my heart and poured out His love for me. And in response, Lord, this is for You.

INTENT AND PURPOSE

The intent and purpose of this book is to impart wisdom and activate people to pray. I want people to believe in the power of and have an advantage in prayer. The prayer strategies in this book are tried and true. I have lived through them and have seen their outcomes. I desire to ignite your prayer life with the same strategies that have ignited mine. This book was created to promote the great and mighty work of a Savior, Deliverer, Provider, and Miracle Worker. Its contents are true. They are there to tell generations to come that He will come if they call. He loves sinners and saints unconditionally, and He can save to the utmost. He can rescue people from every plague, torture, and bondage. He can use ordinary people to bring forth His extraordinary messages. He is the Life Changer, and He has life-changing words. If we are willing, we have the opportunity to experience the phenomenon of prophetic prayer.

INTRODUCTION

"Don't talk to strangers," they would say. And in fact, and theory, this man was a stranger. Even as a child while knowing that strangers were dangerous, this Man provided safety and refuge to my world, which was filled with pain, dysfunction, and confusion. He was different from other strangers. I would cry out by writing letters to Him, asking why: *Why did my mother and father get a divorce? What is going on? Why doesn't my mother like me? What do I do?* All these were questions of a girl who was in pain. Hurt, scared, afraid, and at the age of eight, I sought relief. Little did I know this pain would be the platform for my ministry. And this Man, who started out as a stranger, would soon become so much more.

But wait; the pain wasn't done. It progressed through the early stages of my marriage. I was extremely devoted to my idea of marriage. Like many young ladies, I dreamt about my future with my Prince Charming—like a Cinderella fairy tale. Growing up in a dysfunctional home causes a person to view marriage as a simple convenience and not a sacred vow. I didn't allow that to skew my view of it. Marriage was sacred. But when I entered marriage and was met by more pain, I experienced those same feelings, which had encumbered my life when I was eight years old, and they gave me a shock. It was a shock as radioactive as thunder striking the ground. This shock wasn't destructive; instead, it changed my life and led me to the greatest surrender. This marriage and sacred dream that I had imagined since I was a little girl brought me to my knees as I cried out to God, who was no longer that Stranger. I said, Lord, *I've tried everything to make this marriage work. Help! I need you.*

As I surrendered my life to the Lord, I was supernaturally filled with the Holy Spirit's power, and that is where God began to work on me. Even as a young Christian, my prayer life was extremely valuable to me like precious rubies. I cherished that place of prayer. I didn't know much about prayer, and I hadn't grown up hearing teachings on intercession. The Holy Spirit became my teacher, and I was the student. Fully submitted, the Holy Spirit began to teach me how to relieve the pain that I carried from childhood into my marriage. I found reassurance and comfort in prayer. Many times, when I cried out to God, all I could do was cry. Deep groaning and utterances sprang out of me like living water. These were languages of relief. Lying in this place of prayer and subdued in His presence, I learned where to put this pain. Rising off the floor, I felt as though the heavy load, which I had once carried, didn't feel as heavy anymore.

Even though English was my native language, I preferred to pray in the Spirit because I didn't know what to pray. Prayer was the key. It was the key that unlocked the door to where this long-lasting pain resided. Prayer was the place where I was able to express myself and get the relief that I so desperately longed for. Imagine a cold winter evening. You put a pot roast in the pressure cooker to bring warmth and comfort to the cold wintery night. To properly open the lid, you must slowly release the buildup of pressure first. Then you can lift the lid to look at the pot roast. This is just like life. There must be a release from the buildup of pressure and pain to lift you up. That was what prayer began to do for me; it released the pressure, pain, and agony from my childhood and new marriage.

He is no longer a Stranger. He is my Healer, Deliverer, Way Maker, Shelter, and Teacher. From that point of release on, I began to go to God, consistently seeking Him through prayer and experiencing relief. In God's sovereign wisdom and loving plans, He allowed that place of pain to ignite a hunger in me. I sought knowledge from His Word. I learned who I was in Christ, and that amplification brought me to a deeper revelation of who God was. This process was one of beauty. Like a butterfly grows in its cocoon, I grew in this place of prayer. My focus was no longer on the pain; He became the focus. I got to know Him and His many names. He was no longer a stranger or just my place of relief. This was a phenomenon and a journey, where I learned my superpower: prophetic prayer.

CHAPTER 1

OH, THE PAIN

Is any among you afflicted? Let him pray. (James 5:13 KJV)

THE BIRTH OF DYSFUNCTION

WHILE GROWING UP IN CHURCH, you may have sung the hymn "Amazing Grace." Imagine yourself as a small child walking toward the steeple with your family on a warm Sunday morning. The birds were chirping, Mama was holding your hand, and your brother was kicking rocks along the path. As you approach the building, you hear the choir singing, "Amazing grace, how sweet the sound, that saved a wretch like me."

Well, my walk with Christ wasn't as nostalgic. It was a cold day on February 18 of 1982 when I surrendered my life, heart, and being to God. Let me paint you a picture of a woman who was far too familiar with pain and who reluctantly came to know that Stranger as her Healer. It was like those daily calls from pesky bill collectors, a constant reminder of something I probably needed to give attention to but that I dreaded. But no, it was my friend from school who would persistently invite me to go to church with her. "Come and experience this newfound faith I have," she would say. Week after week, she would call. It never failed.

Then one day, I muscled up the strength to answer the call. I said, "Fine. If I go with you, will you leave me alone?" She humbly replied that she would because she was in on a secret that I wasn't aware of. She knew that the afflicted needed help. My life had malfunctioned, and I needed a fixer—the Fixer—to help me put my life back together. If you've seen anything that depicts the walking dead, it is a factual representation of who I was before I knew Christ. I was afflicted, suffering, in pain, and wrapped in grave clothes. I was suffering under the world's evil treatment. I was in distress, grieved living life in torment, and cast down in soul and mind. I was stricken by evil and troubled on every side. My scars and grave clothes were visible but only to the trained eye. My pain was ever present, as was the harassment from demonic entities. I was like the walking dead. I was looking for something that satisfied the emotions of defeat and mental anguish.

VISITATION OF DEMONIC ENTITIES

I was suddenly awakened, after being asleep. *For what?* I wondered. I was wide awake, so I laid there with my eyes shut, just wondering why. I was around nineteen or twenty years old, unsaved, and single. Still and quiet, I began to hear footsteps coming from my front door to my bedroom. I immediately thought someone had broken into my apartment and that he or she was coming for me. The closer the steps came toward my bedroom, the more afraid I became. I never opened my eyes. A cold presence entered the room without opening the door. The footsteps continued to my bed, and the entity jumped on top of me and sunk into my body. I became paralyzed and speechless as if I was in a vice of some sort. He wrestled with me, reminding me of the man who wrestled with Jacob until the break of day. This was not my first encounter. My first contact happened when I was ten, after going to the movie, *The Night of the Living Dead*. Because of this encounter, I refuse to fund the kingdom of darkness through movies or any other demonic entity that you pay for to be frightened.

My last visitation reappeared early in my ministry, and it was the worst time of wrestling. I was suddenly awakened, wide-eyed, yet still and quiet. Once again, the footsteps in the hallway were getting closer to our bedroom. But this time was different. I wanted, waited, and needed to see. I lifted my head to look and saw nothing. As I lay down, someone or something jumped on top of and stopped me from speaking. It was as if a hand covered my mouth and wrestled with me back and forth to the point of awakening my husband. He thought I was having a nightmare. I was, but in real life. When my husband grabbed me, the entity released me, and I was able to speak again. I am convinced that these visitations were sent as an arsenal against my purpose and destiny.

That arsenal includes fear tactics that decrease our faith and confidence and limit our victories. The phrase "fear not" is used over eighty times in the Bible. Why? Because we are being conditioned to fear our enemies instead of fearing God. The fear of God is the beginning of wisdom and is good for submission, awe, and respect. The purpose of fear from the enemy is to diminish our authority, voice, and capacity. Fear brings torment and timidity, with the intent to war against our faith's confidence, Christ-mindedness, and resistance to sin. David cried, in Psalm 64:1, "Hear my voice, O God, in my prayer, preserve my life from fear of the enemy" (ESV). If God is with us, who can be against us? And if God is for us, whom shall we fear? Let us ask ourselves these questions.

My husband says it like this: Fear is "faith enabled above resistance." Think about it. If you cannot resist the enemy, how will he flee from you? Recall James 4:7 (NIV), where it says to "submit to God and resist the devil, and he will flee from you." That fear came for us as children, with the intent to keep our faith from resisting. Satan knows our faith involves truth, light, and freedom. God will drive out lies, darkness, and bondages.

The enemy is more aware of our call than we are (speaking for myself). We don't just get to this state by simply living. These things are planned to couple with our pain in life and to paralyze us.

The pain that I lived with had an origin—a root that could be traced back to a clear beginning. This is the point when pain became my teacher and tried to be my permanent resident. It started in my childhood. It began with dysfunction. Most of us grew up in dysfunctional homes and in families who loved us based on their own limited, dysfunctional capacities. They, too, did not have the proper love and care that they needed as children, and they were victims of vicious cycles that we all innocently inherited. This cycle produces negative social practices and behavioral patterns that inhibit our ability to grow up and become free, socially sound, and structurally solid. If we never address this pain and introduce it to a Savior who can heal it, we perpetuate this same cycle and give the next generation dysfunctional love, until we decide to fix the malfunction with the ultimate Fixer, the Deliverer who chooses us while we are in our dysfunction.

It was a Valentine's Day that I would never forget. At the age of sixteen, my heart expanded, and it was filled with love for my sweet baby girl. The gift I received on this beloved holiday had been produced through guile and manipulation, which deceitfully tricked me into giving up my virginity at an early age. Now I was broken, afraid, ashamed, and fearing ridicule, which would unknowingly bring me to my knees. I was a child with a child. Abortion immediately became a viable option, but I just couldn't bring myself to feel right about destroying a life. I chose to live with the stigma of being an unwed mother in high school.

I was still in school, and something in me refused to give up and quit. Although I may not have had the language for what that was, I had the drive and tenacity to finish school. In fact, I graduated from high school with honors. I was accepted, and I enrolled in college. This was thanks to my eldest sister, who took care of my daughter for her first two years. She wanted to adopt my baby girl to enable me to focus on school and graduate college. It was a great offer, which I considered. But let me tell you about the loving grace of God, who supernaturally intercepted this decision. A teacher at school spoke to me about giving up my baby girl. This teacher did not know my situation and helped me not to make a choice that I probably would've regretted for the rest of my life. That teacher helped me realize that I did have something to give my baby—and that was me.

Hard life decisions can bring levels of affliction, but you must be true to yourself at all costs. The acknowledgment of trauma and the owning of your pain allow you to break down barriers and resist curses, which can later prevent you from being true to yourself. This truth—your truth—causes a level of comfort and freedom, which is irreplaceable. I am grateful for this truth, but little did I know that I was only at the beginning of rooting out my dysfunction.

THE JOURNEY OF BIRTHING PRAYER

As I was raised in pain and was tutored in dysfunction, it was no shock that these themes transferred to my marriage. I was married at the young age of twenty, having no idea of all that I was getting involved in. I naively carried my bags of hurt, shame, and scars to this new life with my husband. I really began to malfunction as these cycles continued in my life with every changing event. A bit of happiness and laughter shined through the dark, heavy clouds of sadness and pain, at times. Little did I know that this was going to be one of the greatest challenges of my life.

I am grateful for an instrument that God used to bring me to my surrender to Christ. She was a Christian, and she helped me say yes. This vessel was a beautiful demonstration of James 5:13. She prayed for me and saw that I was one of the afflicted ones. She was a living example of 1 Corinthians 3:8, where it says, "Now He that plants and he that waters are one; and every man shall receive his own reward according to his own labor" (KJV). In His awesome wonder, God strategically planted people in my life to pray for me at some of the most trying times of my existence. They intercepted many of the enemy plans as that pertained to my child, marriage, and husband's future.

And that, ladies and gentlemen, is prophetic prayer. We can pray prophetically and not know how the Holy Spirit is using us. He can use us to save another person's life from dysfunction and deadly malfunctions and to bring that individual into a life of freedom and pure joy. This is what He did for me. He has charged me to teach and bring this to others.

But let me go back to James 5:13. What did my affliction look like? I was in deep despair, and I still did not want to step into a church. When I agreed to go with my friend, I did it only so that she would quit harassing me. My reluctant acceptance of a priceless invitation brought me face-to-face with the appointment Giver: Jesus. That Saturday in February felt colder than usual. Despite the initial chill, I was filled with the Holy Ghost's power, with the evidence of speaking in tongues, which produced heat in me that would revolutionize my life forever. I surrendered all the pain that I had been carrying from childhood and marriage. I gave up the fight to be right. Laying down those burdens of affliction and the weight of grief left me with a lightness that shook my being. *What is happening to me? What is this new lightness about me?* I had had a few small dealings with God in past situations, but it was nothing like this.

It was called a new birth. I was in a metamorphosis that had begun the moment I prayed the prayer to accept Jesus as my Lord and Savior. I answered the call to surrender. This experience brought me into a face-to-face meeting, which kept me awake that Saturday night. The relief from those themes and emotions, which had once crowded my life, was now the birthing place for prayer. My eyes were opened. I could now see other afflicted ones. I was no longer consumed with my hurts, but I could see that others needed to experience this same relief. I had a sensitivity to all humankind. I desired for my husband's heart to be healed and for him to experience this same relief.

CLOSING PRAYER

Father God, You are the pain reliever I need for my brokenness, disappointments, struggles, and fears. I believe that only You know the depth of my heart and soul's wounds. I also believe that You are the only One who can bring the fragments of my life to wholeness. During the seasons when pain is my teacher, I pray that I will learn what I need to learn and grow where I need to grow. Thank You that I have the desire to become better, stronger, and wiser through every process. In Jesus's name, I pray.

CHAPTER 2

FROM PAIN TO POWER

And the prayer of faith will save the sick, and the Lord will raise him up ... If he has committed any sins, he will be forgiven and restored. (James 5:15 KJV)

PARTNERING WITH THE HOLY SPIRIT

THE PRAYER OF FAITH IS a clinging and continual wrestling type of prayer. The prayer of faith does not lose heart, but it energizes its own determining force. It's the type of force that pushes past hardships, obstacles, and hindrances. It is fueled by trust and belief in a Savior. It has confidence that Almighty God and Jesus, the Anointed One, are mighty to deliver. He alone is all-powerful, full of wisdom, all-knowing, and always present. This type of prayer is exclusive to partnering with the Holy Spirit.

Three times a day became a theme for my prayer life and the beginning of my journey. Theoretically, I was untrained, but the Holy Spirit, the greatest prophetic Teacher, began to prepare and instruct me for my future ministry. I loved meeting God three times a day. It was as though I was in a new romantic relationship. Like clockwork, a nudging would come, and I would pray. The more consistent I became, the stronger the urge and the greater the contact became. I became devoted to this and enjoyed engaging with the Holy Spirit daily. The Holy Spirit taught me from the book of John, chapters 14–16, how He would stand by, teach, and help me while He was in close fellowship with me throughout my walk.

The Holy Spirit awakened me each night ten-to-fifteen minutes before my husband arrived home. On the floor at my bedside, I prayed only in the Spirit. Imagine my husband walking into the room and seeing no one. He only heard unknown tongues. He later shared that this made him afraid, curious, and desirous all at the same time. Out of fear, he threatened me to stop. But my Partner was steady, persistent, and timely. This continued for several months.

Within six months, my husband surrendered, but the journey there wasn't easy. This partnership with the Holy Spirit was one of extreme devotion and faith. I began leaning and depending more on my Teacher, and His help became vital to my existence. My dependence on Him became my expression through prayer. Like how a baby depends on a mother for food, I became completely dependent and devoted to Him.

Our connection was one like a mother and her babe. In fact, once I started maturing in this partnership, the spirit realm opened up to me. I'd like to caution you that spiritual encounters come from both heaven and hell. Growing in this type of intimacy, you will get visitations from demons and angels. Strange events will happen, like a choir singing behind me, angels standing over me, and demons fleeing from me, to name a few of the encounters that I experienced while praying. I used to have some spiritual encounters as a child, but this was different. This was a very new realm, which came in like a tsunami. I had a new and fresh perspective, mindset, and understanding of the spiritual warfare and battles that I faced as a new believer.

THE ROAD TO RESTORATION

The Holy Spirit wants us to be strategic in our prayers because the enemy also has strategies. He used my husband's pain as a door to persecute me. One night, we were in a heated fight and shouting at each other. Nothing physical! I went upstairs in a desperate attempt to try to avoid him. He followed me up the stairs and insisted on talking to me, when I only wanted to escape the situation. I looked down and saw a knife on the bedroom floor. I wondered how it got there. This was a demonic encounter. The spirit of anger spoke loud and clear to me, *Grab that knife and stab him to shut him down.* In an instant, the Holy Spirit, my Partner and Teacher, clearly said, *It's a trap. Don't do it!!* I stopped in my tracks. I was almost in a trancelike state when I heard both entities (demons & Holy Spirit) speaking. I had a choice to make. Of course, I yielded to the still, soft voice that spoke those words to me.

And the scripture that came to me at that moment was, "What the devil meant for my demise, God turned it for my good" (Genesis 50:20 AMP). Joseph said this to his brothers after going through a very long, painful process. He said it this way: As for you, you meant evil against me, but God meant it for good in order to bring about this present outcome. What outcome was he referring to? Being restored. The power that is reached through pain is restoration. Victory, power, love, forgiveness, and restoration—Joseph's testimony was a phenomenal biblical story of restoration. There was restoration, renewal, and reestablishment to his original, purposeful state. Pain, agony, defeat, unforgiveness, revenge, jealousy, impulses, and urges were replaced with restoration.

When restoration takes place, a new state of mind and heart come into play. New responsibilities and abilities cause a new posture. It's like going into a phone booth as Clark Kent and coming out as Superman. Prophetic prayer mixed with the Word causes the promise of restoration to come to life. Joel prophesied the promise: "I will restore, compensate, to you the years that the locust swarm devoured, the young locust, the other locust and the ravaging locust ... and you shall eat in plenty and be satisfied" (Joel 2:25 ISV). Jeremiah also had a word of promise: "For I fully satisfy the weary soul, and I replenish every languishing and sorrowful person" (Jeremiah 31:25 ESV).

When restoration starts, it gives the revelation of hope, redemption, and covenant. God speaks of a new covenant in Hebrews 8:13: "He makes the first one obsolete, out of use, annulled and growing old, ready to disappear" (ESV). Something has to go to make room for the new so that the new can develop, grow, and be established. When we experience lifting, shifting, replacing, and redemption of our lives, we are restored from the old effects and damages of our former lives and are transitioned or changed into the new. Everything associated with sin, sickness, affliction, disease, and death has been bought by Jesus's blood sacrifice, bringing us back to a former position or condition called restoration.

The power of restoration brings God glory. How does it do this? I'm glad you asked. It happens when we experience restoration through answered prayers and humanity sees and hears of the compassion and love that Father God has for His people. It is His love that has caused everything I've experienced prophetically in prayer. He is a Father who does not falter or fail. But He offers redemption and restoration of our pasts for a greater future. Our greater future is His greater glory. His kingdom is expanding and manifesting. All glory, praise, and honor belong to Him.

God's salvation is inclusive of new and better things to come. But we will never experience all that the Father has for us without intimacy with our Savior. There is no intimacy without communication. Going to church does not qualify us for the restoration of all things.

THE RESTORATION OF REPENTANCE

Engaging with Jesus through the Holy Spirit activates benefits and resources that otherwise would not be at our disposal. It has been proven to be authentic by those who personally engage and are intimately involved with His workings, which is when power is produced. Therefore, when we learn the art of speaking His words first and then watch them transform our world, we speak with greater confidence because we believe and participate in His works of restoration, transformation, and regeneration. In Matthew 12:13, Jesus said to a man whose hand was withered, "Reach out your hand" (AMP), and the Bible says that the man reached out his hand and that it was restored to normal and as healthy as the other. Jesus asked him to participate, partner, and reach. Restoration is significant to regeneration, as in redoing your genes and changing your DNA. So, what is traveling through your bloodline—addictions, diseases, or something else—cannot stop destiny and purpose. The Author and Finisher of our faith is moving earth, flesh, curses, and hell to get us to our destination. It is fascinating.

But the process of our Father's dealings could negate our restoration, if we don't learn to embrace it. We could walk away from His divine plan for us, and that process can turn us back or turn us around. It definitely can bring us to our knees. The prophet Hosea said it like this:

> Come, and let us return to the Lord. For He has torn, but He will heal us. He has stricken, but He will bind us up. And after two days, He will revive us. On the third day, He will raise us up. That we may live in His sight. Let us know, let us pursue the knowledge of the Lord. His going forth is established as the morning. He will come to us like rain, like the latter and former rain to the earth. (Hosea 6:1–3 NKJV)

It is really about knowing and understanding how God processes, establishes, and uses us to refresh and pour out ourselves on the earth and about being born-again. The plan of God births revival, restoration, and a great outpouring globally, which is a good place for repentance. Repentance is turning away from disobedience, rebellion, or sin. It's turning around, going in a new direction, changing one's mind, facing oneself, or just a desperate cry for help. Throughout scripture, there are examples of repentance prayers. One of my favorites is Psalms 51, which was written by David: "Create in me a clean heart, O God, and renew a right spirit within me" (Psalm 51:10 ESV). It covers mercy, lovingkindness, delivering, purging, washing, shaping, and restoring—all components of repentance. Faith turns us toward God and in acceptance of Jesus Christ. This twofold turning of repentance and faith is our entry ticket into the kingdom. Repentance is associated with prayer and intercession because it leads us to a personal Savior and a personal relationship with the God of the universe.

Allow and embrace His dealings to invade your life. Get desperate for change and a life without pain. Let it out. Cry out. All through the Bible, oppressed and depressed people cry out to the true and living God. He answers and listens for the cries of His people. God is in the people business. His compassion and steadfast love for us cause him to give attention to us. Believe it. Receive it. He is paying attention to you.

Now, knowing the history behind my life and all the pain I once bore, I am thankful for the people who prayed for me before I knew how to. That is prophetic. The Holy Spirit is stirring people to pray, intercede, and stand in the gap. We have no idea what is happening behind the scenes for the kingdom of God. We can pray others into their purpose and destiny in Christ while pursuing our purpose and processing our pain.

PROPHETIC PRAYER IS A KEY

People must first be free before they gain a revelation of their purpose and destiny in Christ. There are keys that unlock the mysteries in their lives, and prayer is one of them. Prayer is more for us than it is for God. It is the solution to the problem which brings us closer to the heart of God.

In fact, prayer allowed me to see my husband become free from the grips of darkness. As I was praying, the Holy Spirit began to show me pictures. I received closed visions, which were pictures in my mind. I saw myself standing in front of a large brick wall. My mouth was open and moving as I faced this large wall. As my mouth kept moving, one at a time, bricks began to fall around me. The more I spoke, the more the bricks fell. And at a certain point, I saw a man's head. Then I recognized the man. It was my husband. What did all of this mean? The more that I prayed, the more my husband gained the freedom and ability to move past the brick wall, which had held him captive. It had to fall. Once the wall was removed, he was free to come to Jesus and surrender himself. Two weeks later, he did just that.

This encounter showed me how powerful our prayers can be when they are consistent, focused, and full of faith. As long as my mouth kept moving, the bricks kept falling, but when I stopped speaking, no bricks fell. Keep the prayers of faith that have prophetic power coming. You may not know the impact right away, but I guarantee you, the impact will manifest.

Let's take a moment to stop and think. How many people do you know that are afflicted and in need of someone to pray for them? People are stuck behind their brick walls of bondage, hurt, and pain. They are waiting for prophetic prayers to free them from the entanglements of this life so that they can become productive in God's kingdom. Paul said it like this, "Not that we are fit, qualified and sufficient in our ability of ourselves to form personal judgements or to claim or count anything as coming from us, but our power and ability and sufficiency are from God" (2 Corinthians 3:5 AMP). So I can plant, you can water, but God gives the increase.

What are you bringing forth? What are you sacrificing right now to redeem another person who is afflicted? I urge you not to do this just for you and yours but to realize that there are people who need your gifting, wisdom, and insight into life. Our prayers must be compassionate and selfless and have great concern for the well-being of others. In scripture, Abraham, Moses, and Jesus interceded and petitioned on behalf of others.

As intercessors, we must not build walls that keep people out, but we must be bridges to help people cross. Because we come from such dysfunctional pasts, it is often hard for us to accept the keys of compassion and reach our freedom. We must come to realize that Jesus loves us very much and proves His love regularly. Deuteronomy 31:8 says, "The Lord himself goes before you and will be with you; He will never leave you nor forsake you." He says that He will comfort us in all our troubles (See 2 Corinthians 4 NKJV). He gives us the Holy Spirit, who is the true Comforter, Intercessor, Advocate, and Helper. He is also filled with loving compassion. He is God's representative. He guides and cares for us. He gives us whatever we need and exactly when we need it.

For some time, I couldn't fully imagine having a faith that could change circumstances, let alone the negative thoughts, memories, and scars from my painful past. Yet the Holy Spirit, in His loving compassion, gave me the gift of faith to save me from the negativity that consumed my life. He carries out the will of the Father, and He can do the same for you.

Fellowship with my heavenly Father became so good to me. In His compassionate care and through prayer and intimacy, I gained wisdom. My understanding began to broaden through the study and knowledge of Him and His word. It began small, so don't despise small beginnings. After all, the Word of the Lord says, "On my menservants and maidservants, I will pour out in those days of My Spirit and they shall prophesy. I will show wonders in the heavens above and signs in the earth beneath" (Acts 2:18–19 NKJV).

Oh, yes, and excuses anger God. We can read in Exodus 4:15–16 that when Moses kept telling God about his speech impairment, God told him (I'm paraphrasing), "Let Aaron speak for you, but you have to put the words in his mouth. I, God, will be your mouth, and you put My words in Aaron's mouth, and I will teach you what you are to do. No matter the excuses, the surrender is inevitable."

I remember sitting in the church pew one day. I heard Someone whisper to me ever so softly. I can recall thinking, *Still small voice.* That voice told me, *Give your neighbor money for the offering.* Without question, I graciously sowed into my neighbor's life. Before receiving these keys of prayer and this compassion and knowing His Word, I wouldn't have heard His voice, let alone obey it with such ease. He was strengthening my faith and confidence in hearing His voice, which He does for those who are sincere about learning. Later after the service, my neighbor told me that he did not have an offering. *Wow,* I thought, *Did He just use me like that?* Small consecutive occurrences like this were building up my faith for the greater happenings of God. The Father in His compassionate care was preparing me. The Bible says, "Be faithful in the small things and He will make you ruler of larger things" (Matthew 25:23 ISV). Sometimes, I thought those promptings were just me, but when they came to pass and I received confirmations like that of my neighbor at church, I realized that this was so much bigger than me.

It is only through a real and true relationship with God that we can sense and know He is with us. As my relationship deepened, my life's perspectives began to expand. I was no longer focused only on the negative circumstances and pain from life's happenings. I was becoming more and more liberated in my thoughts and everyday living. Instead of resentment and anger toward people and life itself, feelings of pity left me as hope arose within me. And compassion and healing given by the Holy Spirit began to take me over.

I trust my story may help increase your yearning and desire to use prayer as a key to gain freedom for yourself and others. But I must admit that this newfound relationship does not come without difficulties. It's like a child learning to ride a bike. It's a process that has its ups, downs, bumps, and bruises. Learning to ride this bike would prove harder than I had expected. The freedom from my pain was life changing. I no longer carried a heavy weight, which had skewed my thoughts and perceptions and had perpetuated a seemingly endless cycle of dysfunction. With this newfound freedom, I was ready to rid myself of anything associated with pain, and that brought me to my marriage.

This new experience birthed compassion in me and slowly replaced the anger I had toward my husband. I began seeing his heart instead of focusing on his acts, even though I still lacked the love and energy for my marriage. I knew that inside my husband, there was a well of love and a place where he had been made in God's image and likeness. But still, I began entertaining an unwanted guest. It was something I knew oh so well and never wanted to see again: pain. I cried out to God, sharing my heart with the Father. The Holy Spirit, my Partner, began to inspire me in faith. I spoke confessions of salvation, wholeness, and healing for my husband. Nevertheless, there were no indications that my husband's life was turning around. He seemed to be enjoying his small world of deception. In my mind's eye, which was currently being clouded with pain, I believed his sins to be insurmountable. I was ready to go on with my life and leave him and the pain behind.

Learning to ride a bike can be a difficult task for a young child. At first, we are motivated by the thought of freedom. We ride up and down the city blocks as the wind blows in our face. We try to go faster and faster as we race with our friends. I was like that young child, except I hadn't reached that level of mastery. I was at the point where I constantly fell and bruised myself, which came with the practice of riding a two-wheeled machine. The next time that I fell off the bike was me seeking confirmation to leave my marriage. Don't get me wrong; I had still evolved into an intercessor. I was constantly standing in the gap for my husband and marriage, but I still yearned to be free from it all.

In pursuit of that freedom—riding with the wind in my face and pain behind me—I called my pastor. I poured my heart out over the entire situation. She was very wise, as she listened carefully without saying a word. She was prophetic and heavily endowed by the Holy Spirit. After listening to me go on and on, she finally said, "It sounds like your mind is made up, so I'll just ask this: Can God heal your marriage? And does He want to heal your marriage?" My emotional rant and desperate longing for freedom was brought to an abrupt pause. She gracefully continued with words of wisdom that were so potent, it shook my soul as she spoke. "Along life's way, you will grow and discover more of God. Through that discovery, you will wonder if He could heal it and if it was His will to heal your marriage. But you won't have the answer because you didn't persevere to see what the end might be."

Those words of wisdom resonated in my soul and mind. I heard my Father speaking to me through my pastor that day. Jesus said in John 10:27, "My sheep hear my voice; and I know them and they follow me" (ESV). And that is indeed true. When a father speaks, children stand at attention. Just as a child is acquainted with a father's voice, so are the sheep who have become acquainted with their heavenly Father. There comes a knowing that is born through intimate dealings with the Father. It's like riding a bike. There are constant ups and downs of tasting freedom on that stretch of sidewalk as you get the hang of things, but then painfully, you are brought to your knees after an amateur misstep. But this time, I knew that I was mastering hearing His voice because the words began to minister to my spirit. I fell to my knees and asked for His will. I sincerely wanted to know what His expectations of me were as it pertained to my marriage. I didn't want my marriage, but I found myself concluding my pray with, "Not my will but Yours be done."

CREATED IN HIS IMAGE

As the Father's love heals you, you become more like Him. You are created in His image. His will becomes part of you. In Numbers 12:8, God was speaking directly with His servant Moses "mouth to mouth, clearly, and not in riddles, and he beholds the form of the LORD" (ESV). Generally, we enter into a relationship with God for selfish reasons. Nonetheless, God, in His infinite wisdom, is the master multitasker. He takes our hunger, thirst, and sometimes our selfish desires and draws us nearer so that we can enjoy fellowship with Him. He takes our desires and deals with us on many levels simultaneously. I want to caution you that the more time you spend with God, the more time you will want to spend with Him and become like Him. Before long, the Holy Spirit's inspired prayer produced a deep yearning in me to see my husband accept Christ and adopt His will, just as I had done. I unexpectedly became hopeful and inspired. It wasn't a selfish hope for my husband and me but for him and the Father to meet and commune. I was subtly taken out of the picture. It was no longer my will being done, but my Father's will.

Many of us had to be taught to ride a bike, or maybe you've taught a child to ride. While teaching, sometimes certain adjustments must be made. When beginners ride, they may lean too far to one side or have a problem steering. Sometimes it takes a parent coming, adjusting their postures, and helping them get on the right track. I needed an adjustment. I needed an increase in faith.

Over the next few days, I continued to ask the Lord for confirmation to leave my marriage. One day, he answered me in one statement, *This is your husband.* I stopped and immediately asked, *What does that mean?* I had no clue what He meant, but I was surely about to find out. As I began to meditate on God's Word, I began to recognize what He was saying. It began to reshape my mind and perspective. He was saying, *The choice is yours. You can either stay or go. Which will you choose? Just know, My will is that he is your husband.* He was laying it all in my lap. In simple terms, he said that it was His choice for me and wanted to know what I would do.

I needed to settle the restlessness in my thoughts, emotions, and feelings. But how? I needed to repeat what God was saying and come into agreement with it. My faith needed to increase. Like the apostles said to Jesus in Luke 17:5, "Increase our faith [our ability to confidently trust in God and in His power]" (AMP). I needed to accept His will in my heart and boost my trust in what God was saying to me. I needed to recognize that as I was being trained as an intercessor, a tower was being built. It wouldn't feel good, but ultimately, it would be worth it. My mind was being renewed through the Word and prayer. As the dust settled, I nursed my wounds just as a small child who is learning how to ride a bike does. I got back on that bike, and I rode. I recognized that as I was strengthened and as I moved with the Holy Spirit, the wind began to carry me through.

What did this mind renewal look like? Well, mentally and physically, I began to pack up my marriage just as one does before embarking on a move into one's new home. I had to gradually unpack those boxes mentally and physically. I beautified my home with His words. I wrote out scriptures, cut them out, and taped them over doors, mirrors, and walls throughout my home. I was like a child learning new words. I became hungry and desperate to see His will come to pass in my life, so I searched for every promise that applied to daily situations. Each room that I painted with scriptures told of a renewed and restored story in my life. It was the complete opposite of what I had previously known.

Some may think that this is a little juvenile, but I was truly like a baby learning how to walk, with my hand in the hand of my Father. I was embracing His dealings and happenings just as a growing toddler trusts the safety of his or her parents' embrace and puts one foot in front of the other while leaning on the strength of the parent. And just as those parents affirms their child's attempts, God honored my effort. What was my reward? Every promise came to pass in a timely manner. I didn't know the scriptures well, but I didn't have to because the Holy Spirit did.

Within six months, my husband gave his life to the Lord, and he was filled with the Holy Spirit. He wasn't the only one being transformed. Even in that amount of time, a power of raw energy had risen inside of me. What emerged was confidence. It replaced the pain, sorrow, and pity that had torn me down for so many years. The pain wasn't completely gone, but it no longer ruled my life. My faith had been rewarded. I experienced an internal power that had drowned out the pain; its presence was barely known. These prayers of faith had literally healed the sick. It wasn't only my prayers but those of partners, leaders, counselors, and the family of God—there were many prayers. And the tongues of the wise brought healing (See Proverbs 12:18 NIV).

We must understand that God, our Father, can heal pain instantly and leave no trace of it. However, when He chooses to take us through a process instead, there is always a lesson in the pain and the presence of it. The presence of pain can make us do some terrible things and cause us to morph into someone that we don't recognize. So the Father will use the process to slowly walk us through lessons, overcome the trauma of our pasts, and allow time for us to learn our renewed selves. When our minds are being renewed daily, we no longer focus on those areas of pain, and faith is born. Just like after days of practice, bumps, and bruises, when we finally get the hang of riding that glorious two-wheeled bike, we begin to peddle with a renewed sense of confidence and ride with freedom as the wind hits our faces. We feel reborn, and we come alive.

> And the prayer of faith will restore the one who is sick, and the
> Lord will raise him up; and if he has committed sins, they will
> be forgiven. (James 5: 15, NASB)

I literally lived this scripture out in living color. It was for my husband, and it was for me. I was born again. I shed that familiar heaviness of pain and put on the garments of praise and power.

FREEDOM FOR ALL

Three times a day was now a definite theme for my prayer life. As the Holy Spirit tutored me in prophetic prayer, strategies were implemented, which will be mentioned throughout the next chapters. So look for them to enhance your prayer life. Each morning, I would get my daughter off to school and begin singing, praising, and entering into His courts. I allowed the Holy Spirit to take over. As I spoke in tongues with my eyes closed, I focused on a picture in my head. Sometimes I would picture the cross or focus on the name of Jesus in bold lettering, which was written on the cross. Using these sorts of images helped me to close out the noises and cares of the world.

Then by the afternoon and before my daughter came home from school, there was another pause. I shut the TV off, read something in scripture, and allowed the Holy Spirit to lead the most skilled teacher and prayer partner. Nighttime was the best time for prayer. The house was quiet, and everyone was fast asleep. I would just get lost in worship. High praise was in my mouth, and my hands were lifted as I allowed the Holy Spirit to take control. Giving the Holy Spirit full reign makes greater room for the prophetic during prayer. It helps me reach higher heights and deeper depths spiritually. This is the epitome of adding super to our natural and bringing the supernatural to our neighborhoods, lives, and the world.

What is apparent in all of this is simple: consistency. Jehovah Rophi is a Healer. The prayer of faith should not waver. You must learn to contend and wrestle with it. This prayer is not easily given up or turned over because you have lost heart. This type of prayer will energize you as you become more and more determined in God's confidence. This prayer trusts and believes. It is assured with confidence that God the Father, Jesus our chief Cornerstone, is mighty to save, heal, deliver, and provide wisdom for any and every situation in life. James gave us an example in James 5:10, "Take, my brethren, the prophets, who have spoken in the name of the Lord, for an example of suffering affliction, and of patience (KJV).

Closing Prayer

Father God, You raised me out of a bed of affliction to a place of peace and power, where I can exchange torment for perfect peace in my mind. It is a place of power where sin cannot rule me, hatred cannot school me, and circumstances cannot fool me. My newfound faith has inspired me. It has been refined into a living faith that ignites my spirit to overcome and reach for a restored life in Christ because I have been bought, sealed, and delivered through the resurrection of my Lord and Savior, Jesus Christ.

CHAPTER 3

THE LIFE OF GAIN

That I may gain Christ and be found in Him. (Philippians
3:8–9 NIV)

Recognizing that the power you possess is a gift from God the
Father is essential. Neither I nor anyone in the body of Christ walks in the
full power that Christ intended for us. We were called to live at a high level
of power and authority. Just think about the life of Christ in the gospels.
He operated at a high level of supremacy and authority. And in that, He
promised whosoever believed "greater works." John 14:12 says "Truly,
truly, I say to you, whoever believes in me will also do the works that I do;
and greater works than these will he do, because I am going to the Father
(ESV). Just think about it: *greater works*. What do you think you must do
to achieve those greater works? How do you access that level?

Fundamentally, we must first know the person we are and what we are
called to do. Then we must understand and become skilled at our craft—
coming into the full knowledge of the power and authority that has been
given to us. Then we must study our gifts and understand what it attracts
and is stimulated and inspired by. This is the road we must take to greater.

These are the steps to obtain this kind of power. This road and these steps are the life of gain. It is a beautiful exchange of what we once knew for a new level of power, authority, understanding who we are, and the level of impact we were called to.

For every new convert who is living by faith and witnessing, faith's rewards are a true gift from God. This process is necessary, and we need to go through it. For some, it can be difficult. Personally, I didn't focus on this process because the privilege was mind-blowing. The new relationship was interesting and exciting. I was on a honeymoon with the Father. I delighted myself in Him as I learned the person I was in this life of gain.

Focusing on Christ makes any process go faster. Think of an athlete's training. Successful athletes must go through rigorous training, which may seem endless, but to make it through, they don't focus on the pain, but they focus on the gains. Focusing on the pain of the process can paralyze them, so they choose to focus on the gain that comes with the training. There are literal gains, such as muscle and speed, and mental gains, such as fortitude and stamina.

That was where I was. What mattered to me was the peace, joy, and new life that became evident in my very being. The warfare I experienced while praying for my husband no longer brought me to a place of exhaustion. Peace kept me in my place of prayer and intercession as I stood solid and watched Christ fight my battles. Don't be mistaken, there were times I would feel the impact of the battle, but it didn't move me. The faith I received like that in Luke 17:5(ESV), held me, and I was not shaken. My spiritual dad always said, "Let the main thing be the main thing." This message was very good and always stuck with me. That was exactly what I was doing. I no longer emphasized the pains of the process. I let the love and sheer delight of my new relationship with Father God sustain and drive me. This is the main course of our life of gain: letting His words and presence make the difference in our lives as we gain new strength and authority, which will make the difference in our worlds and the world of others as we intercede.

In this life of gain, it is similar to the beginning of a new relationship between two people. I was content, excited, and anticipating a lasting journey. And in the journey, my Lover, Christ, began to reveal gifts to me. Along with peace, strength, and joy, I began to learn more about my specific calling. In Mark 8, Jesus called His disciples together and gave them a principle of gain as they walked with Him. He taught them that they must deny themselves, meaning they must set aside selfish interests, take up their crosses, and endure whatever came. We must follow Him and conform to His example in living and suffering. The disciples laid down their previous lives and gained a life with Christ.

PROPHETIC GAIN

When I read Jeremiah 27:18, it blessed me. It says, "But if they are Prophets, and the word of the Lord is with them, let them now make intercession to the Lord of Hosts" (ESV). No one had taught me about the prophetic. It wasn't being preached during that time period. Mostly, we heard messages on faith, where people taught that you could hear from God and that God was speaking, but they never discussed prophets and the prophetic. Nevertheless, I began to see pictures in my mind's eye; like the one of my husband, behind the brick wall and bricks falling as I spoke or pictures of someone and knowing what to specifically pray for them. The Holy Spirit began to teach me, and I gained so much insight and foresight—that was my life of gain. I began to gain a proper perspective on life and love. I loved the sinner and the saint. I wanted to be a solution and not a problem. I wanted to share Christ, my Savior, with everyone who did not know Him. I counted my past as lost. No more chains were holding me. I laid down my previous life of pain for this new life of gain.

It took one year for the Holy Spirit to heal my emotions, cares, worries, and blockages. I gained a new language, which I didn't fully understand. This language gave me an advantage. Instead of cussing, fussing, and trying to convey my emotions in the flesh, my new language began to articulate something deeper and genuine: my heart for God. In this new language, He listened and considered my every word. Just like the freshness of a relationship that is everlasting, God was intentional and endearing as I became acquainted with Him and His ways. I was transformed, and my shell was broken. The more I learned, the more I wanted to share it. It's like when you find that great sale. It's so good that you almost don't believe it. As you rack up the bargains, you eagerly text and call any friend who will listen. That is exactly what I did. I shared Christ with *everyone*, especially my husband. Initially, he listened with disbelief. I could tell he was thinking, *This sounds too good to be true—and it probably is.* He was wrong.

My new gained power was achieving serious momentum. The Holy Spirit was an amazing Teacher. Each day, He would awaken me ten minutes before my husband's arrival. He instructed me to pray in the Spirit and continue there for fifteen or more minutes after my husband arrived home. This continued for days and even weeks, as I vigorously aggravated the spiritual realm, where I was threatened, mocked, and ridiculed. As I listened to the enemy's mockery, I asked the Lord if He heard what was going on. Clear as ever, I would hear Him speak, *Continue to pray.* And that is exactly what I did. Like clockwork, the prayer continued.

Admittedly, the Holy Spirit had me doing other creative things like anointing my husband's underwear, socks, shoes, and T-shirts with oil. I would pray over them. He knew nothing about it, and later, he told me that he was becoming afraid of me and that he no longer knew who I was. He was encountering Christ, and nothing about that was familiar. He conceded later that I wasn't playing fair and that he didn't have a chance to fight back with the power and authority from my new life of gain.

A SOUL GAINED

After six months of operating in this new life, my husband did a 180-degree turnaround. He was hungry and thirsty for Christ, fully surrendered, and gaining Christ. When I laid down my life, I not only gained Christ but also gained my husband, who was a new creation. His testimony is because of the drastic changes in my life. He became thirsty for the living water that I was drinking. Although he was afraid of me and the things I was doing, he desired the same thing. I didn't quench the Spirit and gave Him free speech. The Holy Spirit is all wisdom, and no one can come except if that person is drawn to Him. My husband's salvation was always in the heart of God. He just needed someone to stand in the gap on his behalf. He needed an intercessor—someone who was in Him and had the prophetic posture of what only He could see. My journey with Christ has proven to be the greatest gain of my life.

Everything in my life before Christ has become a blur. It is like taking a road trip up a mountain. Once you reach the top, everything is behind you, and the long strenuous roads all become a blur. The journey that never fully satisfied you and the portions of the mountain that were never enough are all a blur. This is how it is in my own life. The places and people whom I tried to fit in with and never connected to my purpose became a blur. Artificial life supports that I had allowed to pacify me in tough moments were a blur. I had searched for true support and stability through relationships, career choices, sex, alcohol, and parties, but all this was futile. Why? Because my purpose of living was far greater. There was a part of life that I hadn't experienced. God had a greater advantage that I had not tapped into yet.

> But what things were gain to me, those I counted loss for
> Christ. Yea doubtless, and I count all things but loss for the
> excellency of the knowledge of Christ Jesus my Lord: for whom
> I have suffered the loss of all things, and do count them but

dung, that I may win Christ, And be found in him, not having mine own righteousness, which is of the law, but that which is through the faith of Christ, the righteousness which is God by faith. Phil 3:7–9 (KJV)

For His sake, I have lost everything. This is a natural and spiritual loss. I consider it all garbage so that I may gain Christ and be found in Him. My Lord had wooed me with an appetite for greater things. He gave me a desire for deeper things so that I was no longer satisfied by artificial love, support, or systems. So, I willingly let that past life go. It was a blur in the rearview mirror of my travels. The higher I went in Him, the more my past blurred behind me.

The more you recognize that there is more for you to have, peace and joy begin to define you. The garbage you once held onto, which made you feel small, lost, or insignificant is exchanged for meaning, purpose, and destiny. All the energy that I once put into unforgiveness, toxic relationships, and ungodly behavior was put into Christ's hands. I learned that I had to become disciplined. To find my true self and gain identity, I had to trust, rely on, reach, and seek deeper in Him. The person you are has nothing to do with religion and everything to do with faith.

MISTAKEN-BELIEF RELIGION

There is no true heart connection in religion. Religion lacks affection, passion, vision, worship, and truth. What religion isn't void of is mundane practices and appearances. It is just dead works. Religion can never be found in intimacy. It can never follow, obey, or be found in Him. (See Isaiah 29:13 NIV). A heart that is away from God is religion. A heart that is drawn to Him is a life of gain.

Religion is a set of human-made practices, which are designed to give you status. It seeks its own recognition. Because its contents are made by humans, it lacks a true connection to Him. It leaves its followers feeling empty and unfulfilled. They have no allegiance or dependency on anyone. Religion is a tool of divisiveness in the body of Christ. A true relationship is what really fulfills. It is like a mother giving birth to an infant. That infant needs closeness with and is dependent on the nurturer. Without them, an infant feels empty, lifeless, and deficient. True closeness and dependency with our Father causes us to be filled with love, acceptance, honor, appreciation, confidence, and self-respect. These are things that humans and religions can't give or take away once received. Religion depletes confidence, but relationship adds and multiplies confidence.

Where do we start building relationships? We start with communication. Just like a new couple has to navigate the waters through conversation, the same is true of our fellowship with Christ. Prophetic prayer is praying in faith the scriptures under the inspiration of the Holy Spirit to bring God's kingdom and His will to the earth realm. It teaches us how to pray strategically through declarations, decrees, and commands to bring break through. The prophetic produces a powerful connection to intercessory prayer, giving us the ability to see the future. When we have a prayer life, we gain a Christ life. He becomes our Head, leading, directing, engaging, organizing, and holding our lives together.

God is not impressed with how much you do or don't know. He isn't concerned with the size of your vocabulary or comprehension. He is only focused on your communion with Him.

> I come in faith believing that He is and He is a rewarder of those that diligently seek Him. (Hebrews 11:6 NKJV)

I came to God empty and knowing nothing, except that He was able to save. Now I am filled, postured, and purposeful. Through this type of communion, I am joining Him, His will, His way, His joys, His peace, and His strength. Gaining Him becomes the focus and not the process of aimless wandering through life with no substance.

CLOSING PRAYER

Father God, help my faith so that I might gain the privilege and advantage of knowing my Lord and Savior, Jesus Christ, the anointed One, intimately. He is the One who anoints me for service and fills me with joy that is incomparable to anything this world has to offer. It allows me to be found solid in Jesus, with genuine faith and a righteous character, which comes from Him alone. May that be my payment for the losses in my life, and may it always be forever. In Jesus's name.

CHAPTER 4

INTERCESSION AT ITS FINEST

Confess your faults to one another and pray for one another. (James 5:16 KJV)

INTERCESSOR AS A CLOSER

THERE USED TO BE A show on television called *The Closer*. If you're like me, you enjoy suspenseful shows filled with episodes about medicine or the law. In particular, this show was special because the main character was extremely skilled at closing sensitive, high-profile cases, which proved too difficult for others. Episode after episode, the CIA trained specialist not only solved cases but also obtained confessions that led to even more convictions. When things needed to be solved, they called her, the Closer.

I believe that this show provides a beautiful analogy of what it means to be an intercessor. Intercessors are called to be closers, to handle highly sensitive cases, and to bring them to a positive end. Intercessors have a unique skill that allows them to resolve cases that are sometimes seemingly lost. Through our intercession, we resolve sensitive circumstances. We are closers.

Prayer is the key to survival in the life of an intercessor. But the inspiration of an intercessor is love. The sacrifice of this love adds to the uneasiness of the call. And the call consists of praying for others. We intervene, negotiate, and arbitrate to save their lives or to stand in the gap on their behalf.

It was nighttime, and I was praying. As I prayed, I kept seeing a picture of the couch in our living room. My husband was in the bathroom, but once he came out, I shared what I saw. Together, we decided to go and pray for the couch. Logically, we didn't know what was about to happen, but we were obedient to the leading of the Holy Spirit. Sometimes we may not know what the Holy Spirit is trying to make known to us, but we must surrender our logic and trust Him.

We both knelt and laid our hands on the couch. Not totally understanding but in obedience to the vision I saw, I said, "We are here, Lord, to pray." When the words left me, my eyes were closed, but I could feel the hair on my arms stand straight up. The room grew cold. A presence was there. I did not see my husband, but the Holy Spirit became intense during prayer. This cold presence in the room flew off the couch, hit a window, and left. After the presence left, I turned to look for my husband. He was in a fetal position and crying profusely on the floor. Something broke; it was the cry of freedom. Prophetic prayer had broken us from it. We were freed from an entity that was there to afflict us. Prayer can uncover demonic forces and cast them out. No stronghold is safe or secure when we operate in prayer's manifesting power. There is a phenomenon in prayer, and it even affects the smallest things in our lives. It leaves a lasting impact, just like it did for us that day while praying at our couch. Prayer saved my husband's life and mine. We stood in the gap as closers, and God was faithful. He brought freedom.

Jesus was our example of an intercessor (closer). Isaiah 53:12 tells us that He made intercession for transgressors, rebels and violators of God's will. Without Christ's intervention or interceding on our behalf, we wouldn't be here today. This is when we see that intercession is vitally needed. Another term for intercession is standing in the gap. As intercessors, we are called to be like Christ. We are to stand in the gap for the lost, the backslider, or those who just need a helping hand from God. Just like the apostle Paul said in Romans 14:13, "Do not judge one another but resolve" (NKJV). In other words, we should be a part of the solution to other people's issues, closing them out to bring a divine resolution. We are not to put a stumbling block in other people's way or to cause them to fall. In Hebrews 7:25, we read, "He is also able to save to the uttermost those who come to God through Him since He ever lives to make intercession for them" (KJV). Through intercession, we make a difference like Christ did, have an influence like Christ had, and make divine calls as we bring souls to Him because it is He who can save to the utmost.

People who don't have a relationship with God need a bridge by which they can reach Him. Imagine the Golden Gate Bridge in California, except picture that the bridge is not fully constructed. There are two bodies of land separated by water with no way to the other side. People with no connection to God live on the side without access to Christ and have no way of reaching Him. Intercessors act as builders, constructing the bridge of access through their prayers. Once the bridge is complete, intercessors are the vehicle. God is the driver, and our prayers help reach that person and bring them across. We close the gap, intercede, and get a stranded soul to a place where it is now able to commune with God, and this is a beautiful thing. We stand in Jesus's stead. They may not know or see Him, but we act as His proxy, and they learn Him and who He is through their interactions with us. We are the bridge—the connection. In our prayers and intercessions, we don't need to know the details of their circumstances (unless He reveals it), but we consistently pray until that bridge is built, and we close the gap.

Praying for others in this fashion is like Jesus in Luke 23:34: "Father, forgive them, for they do not know what they do" (ESV). He said this to those who were crucifying Him. As you continue reading in that chapter, the two criminals who were having a conversation while being hung with Him had two different perspectives. To the one who asked Jesus to remember him, His answer was that for certain, that day, he would be with Him in Paradise. Jesus is your bridge, your connection, and the door that you may enter to be with Him throughout eternity. Jesus prophetically became a closer to one of the criminals. Jesus is the spirit of prophecy. (See Revelations 19:10) He knew the power of intercession, building, and making it a phenomenon on the cross.

THE MOTIVATING FORCE: LOVE

All intercessors must have a motivating force and a driving influence behind their prayers. Jesus's inspiration behind His intercession was His love for humankind. The strongest evidence of one's love for another is the level of personal sacrifice that one is willing to make. Looking to Jesus as the perfect example, He made the ultimate sacrifice. In Luke 22:32, we find that He interceded on behalf of Peter and His disciples. His greatest example of love in prayer is the continuous intercession and pleading He does for Christians in Romans 8:26–27.

Another example of love in prayer is Samuel's powerful statement in 1 Samuel 12:23, which says, "As for me, far be it from me that I should sin against the Lord by failing to pray for you" (NIV). Here, we see his life of prayer and sacrifice lived out. Failing to do so was sinning against the Lord. We read that Samuel's life of prayer affected God to the point of national revival. Even King David was birthed through Samuel's prophetic intercession. These prayers affected God because He couldn't deny Himself. He swears by no other. He is the ultimate and sovereign One.

Sacrifice isn't always easy. It requires a particular level of selflessness.

Earlier, I shared about the brick wall that I saw in a closed vision as I prayed for my husband. I had to keep speaking to the wall until it crumbled. There were six months of consistent intercession before that wall actually fell down. Intercession is not for the fainthearted. We cannot get weary when the results of our prayers aren't instant. Being self-consumed will cause us to lose sight of the results of our prayers. We must consistently speak to it and understand that our words are spirit and life. They create us and navigate us through life, by encouraging, building, and comforting us as we speak through the Spirit's inspiration.

As a prophetic intercessor, I recognize that I was saved to intercede for the people I love and care for. In Ezekiel 22:30, the Bible tells us that God sought a man among them who would make a wall and stand in the gap before the Lord on behalf of the people. I am called to intercede on behalf of the conditions and affairs of our nation. I pray for the president, the decision-making bodies, and the body of Christ. I understand my assignment as a prophetic intercessor. My assignment is to go before God and to seek reconciliation between Him and His creation (See 2 Corinthians 5:18–20 KJV). It is my desire to be compassionate, selfless, and have a true concern for the well-being of others.

If we as intercessors take our places, I sincerely believe that there are enough genuine, authentic intercessors to close every gap. Together, we can repair or rebuild every broken-down place and heal every broken heart, all over this nation. Fraudulent intercessors cannot or will not stand in the gap. They only follow their hearts and not the heart of the Father. I must ask how available are you? Do you understand the assignment? I am exhorting and urging you like Paul exhorted Timothy in 1 Timothy 2:1–2, when he said, "Therefore I exhort first of all that supplications, prayers, intercessions and giving of thanks be made for all men, all kings and all who are in authority, that we may lead a quiet and peaceable life in all godliness and reverence" (KJV).

PRAYER PARTNERS AND CONFESSIONS

Intercessors have skills to connect, liberate, and move in ways that may seem difficult for others to understand. Remember *The Closer*. She skillfully closed cases through confessions. What I enjoy most about watching some of these lawyer shows is how the detectives work seamlessly with their partners. They come in with a strategy that the suspect is oblivious to. After pointed questions and finesse, they get the confession. Closers bring those who are not connected to Christ to confession. And yes, the intercessor needs to confess. Intercessors are closers, praying the lost in so that they see the need to confess and come to Christ.

We are on call 24-7. At any moment or time of day, we can be led to pray on behalf of another. And if there are times we can't pray, we must have others who can stand and cover us. Ecclesiastic 4:9–10 says, "Two are better than one because they have a good reward for their labor. For if they fall, the one will lift up his fellow: but woe to him that is alone when he falls; for he hath not another to help him" (ESV). Every intercessor should have a partner; it is a good idea.

Do you have a prayer partner? Jesus said that if two believers on Earth agree, in one mind and in harmony, about anything and ask within the will of God, it will be done for them by my Father in heaven. For where two or three are gathered in His name, meeting together as followers, He is there among them (See Matthew 18:19–20 KJV). We bring heaven to Earth through prayer and agreement. Praying for one another is an arsenal of weaponry that can take our enemies out and shut down their operations. You need someone who believes the way you do and exercises faith and trust in the Father above all else.

I believe the body of Christ has overlooked prayer partners. They are a strategic plan that we have overlooked in scripture. Prayer partners plow through the enemy's schemes and produce a fierce power of agreement and strength, which can be applied against the devil's kingdom. The devil knows teamwork better than we do, so we must become strategic and wise.

The devil uses tactics of isolation, convincing us that we are the only ones going through certain things.

Over the years, I have had many prayer partners. Some relationships worked while God used others as a lesson. Even the process of simply seeking out a prayer partner taught me so much regarding strategic prayer. This process requires trial and error. I learned that the formula for a balanced prayer partner was that each person in the relationship had to demonstrate fruit in his or her own life of prayer and have some knowledge of prayer. At a minimum, that person had to show interest in learning more about prayer. Prayer requires a proper fit and flow, so a partner must be consistent, spiritual, and versatile in prayer. Each one brings his or her gifts, perceptions, and approaches to prayer. When both people are dependable and precise, schedules and responsibilities will not hinder that place of prayer. It is vital to make time to pray together and for each other.

I discovered this scripture through one of my prayer partners. She is very knowledgeable of the Word. Malachi means my messenger. I love that acknowledgment of two believers having respectful conversations. Because they fear God and meditate on His Word, He listens and remembers. He hears, records, and remembers their honor, loyalty, and faith. Malachi 3:16 says, "Then those who feared the Lord talked often one to another; and the Lord listened and heard it. A book of remembrance was written before Him. For those who fear the Lord and who meditate on His name" (KJV).

Another powerful weapon that we have at our disposal is confession. Remember that in The Closer, she would get the hard cases solved by getting suspects to confess. The original text for the word *confess* in Greek *Exomologeo* means to acknowledge, agree fully, profess, or promise openly. The original text for the word *fault* in Greek *Paraptoma* means a deviation, error, transgression, fall, offense, trespass, sin, or lapse (See James 5:16). Our enemy uses our faults and fault finding as tactics of isolation, secret sins, and guilt to keep us in bondage. Confession is a place of power and deliverance, where resolution can come forth. It works as therapy when we can acknowledge our perceptions and ideas of ourselves. As an intercessor, we are like Jesus. We do not take the infirmities of others upon ourselves because Christ already did that (See Matthew 8:17). Through prayer, we can take them off others and put them where they belong: under the law and in hell.

James encourages us to "confess our faults." To do this, we must become vulnerable and engage with each other's difficulties. Everyone has fleshy works to overcome and conquer. Being an intercessor and praying with a partner helps to ensure that each intercessor is covered and that he or she can overcome every battle. This is a place of deliverance. It's not just the intercessor taking the faults, weaknesses, and offenses of others but of one another too. Now we know that Jesus is our High Priest (See Hebrews 4:15) and that we have direct access to God the Father when confessing sins.

2 Corinthians 1:10–11 says, "He has delivered us from such a deadly peril, and He will deliver us again. On Him we have set our hope that He will continue to deliver us, as you help us by your prayers. Then many will give thanks on our behalf for the gracious favor granted us in answer to the prayers of many" (NIV). We see that we are not to do this with just anyone, but we all must find that person whom we can be vulnerable with and allow those confessions to come forth, to help with our deliverance. We take our sins to Jesus alone and not to a mere human. But if we lack the know-how or a relationship with our high priest, we may very well need the help of someone else.

It is a great danger to our walk when we cannot openly expose areas of weaknesses, transgressions, faults, or errors. They are called secret sins because we hide or keep them private. These secret sins can become strongholds and corruption in our lives. The enemy uses these secret sins as doorways so that he can come in and out of our lives and cause us to deviate from our destiny, purpose, and the will of the Father.

It can distract us from our place of prayer and cause us not to operate as effective intercessors. I have known sinners and saints who pretend that they are put-together, good people with nothing going on. You know the typical masks that many wear. Before long, you see the impact of the struggle to maintain this mask, and sadly, many fall or lapse into deep dark areas, which they never intended to partake of. Sin is sin, but hidden sins cause more damage and casualties. These hidden faults create barriers, condemnation, deep-seated prisons, and bondages.

Bringing that sin to light through confession causes the rats of depression, anger, lust, and anything else that we may be facing to scatter. This is a place of deliverance. In Psalm 36:9, David put it like this: "In your light we see light" (NIV). You won't know what's lurking in the darkness until the light shines on those hidden places. Only God can reveal the deep and secret things. He is the one who knows what is lurking in the darkness, and He is the Light Giver. Through His light, we can confess the way that David did—a threefold cord of repentance in Psalm 51:1–17: first, my transgression and open rebellion; second, my iniquity and deception of a hidden sin; third, my sin and broken fellowship with the Father. David said that he had sinned against God alone. Many of us know that our confessions don't need to be given to another person. But because the devil uses the tactics of isolation, condemnation, shame, and guilt, we need to become accountable, reachable, and unified.

I caution you not to be deceived by hiding places or the hidden things in your soul. God already knows what is there, and He sees it. He will allow you to hold onto your darkness, if that's what you want. My spiritual dad used to say that the Holy Spirit is a gentleman. He will never snatch what you want to hold onto. So open your mouth and confess the dark stuff.

In the same way you confessed that Jesus is your Lord and that He died for your sins, you must do that here. When we confess our faults to one another, we receive hope and answers that will never come in that hidden place. God never intended for us to be alone. In fact, He said it was not good for humans to be alone. He wants us to be a part of an intimately close relationship (1 John 1:7 KJV).

This is something we must practice. It will not come easy for most. Many of us have to work through years of trust issues, fears, hurts, and wounds from our pasts. If you are in that category, ask God to open your eyes and heart to practice this so that you can become a healthier member of the body of Christ. This will move us into our purpose and destiny. It will help us grasp the distinction our lives are called to and enable us to slay the giants in our lives and the lives of others.

STANDING IN THE GAP FOR OTHERS

Accepting the call as an intercessor should not be taken lightly because it is no easy charge. There will be times when you are fervently praying on behalf of another person while simultaneously standing against the evil works that the very ones you are praying for are throwing at you.

As you've read, this was the case with my assignment to pray for my unbelieving husband. Before his transformation, he lived as he pleased, as we all do. Many of his actions were hurtful, and it was difficult for me to witness God's transference of love and compassion for my husband. Despite my feelings of hurt, I prayed and cried out for his life. Becoming steady in this didn't come seamlessly. I had to create and live within a prayer schedule. To be consistent, I daily communed with God and the Holy Spirit. I also fasted, faithfully attended service, learned the Word, and fellowshipped with believers of like faith. This brought strength to my life and steadied me for this assignment.

Now, don't get it twisted. My works did not replace grace, but instead, they proved that I truly had faith. My flesh was weak, but my spirit was willing to remain steadfast. Being a closer or intercessor, who is called to bring about salvation and deliverance for a life, is never easy. I didn't necessarily enjoy being awakened all those nights and commissioned to pray for my husband, whom I also had conflict with, but intercession isn't an easy call. Ultimately, it is worth it.

Beware because the adversary hates it when we pray for one another. He will try every tactic to cause you to come down from your post and relinquish your assignment. The enemy tried to bring strife and every evil work to stop me. We must know that our power is the key to combat every enemy spirit and take back territories that have been given to us. There are situations around you that God is waiting to partner with you in. God needed a prayer partner to bring my husband to the place he belonged, and that happened when I found my place in the gap.

You may be thinking, *Yeah, that seems easy when it's your husband you're praying for.* Well, my husband isn't the only soul whom I've had to stand in the gap for. On two separate occasions, I prayed, and it saved lives. Only a few months apart, two babies were both saved from abortions through prophetic intercession. I often prayed for people I knew or met along life's paths. I recall one particular day that was different. Early that morning, I was on my way to pick someone up. I drove as I normally did, and I wasn't considering the route more than I usually did. But as I drove past the abortion clinic, I looked up and saw a familiar person going in. I asked the Holy Spirit what I should do. He immediately told me to call a person who was a close contact to the person I saw. I called that person and told her what I had just witnessed and asked her for help. The Holy Spirit used her to drive to the clinic and talk to that person. After their brief talk, they left the clinic that day together, untouched. Later in May, the baby was born. The baby is now a healthy adult. I often lifted up these people in my prayer times. I believe that morning, I ran an interference for God, who put me at the right place at the right time.

The other account was the same year. I was awakened around 6:00 a.m. As I lay there, I began to recall the vivid dream I had had. I dreamed that someone I knew very well was pregnant. I had no prior knowledge that she was pregnant. I had not heard any rumors of it. I just had this dream. In the dream, she denied that she was pregnant, even though to me, it was clear that she was. She tried to leave the place where we were, and I fought to detain her. By 7:00 a.m., I called this person to talk. She immediately became defensive and asked why I would call her that early in the morning, asking questions. I began to tell her about the dream, and she thought I had made it up. I plainly asked her, "Are you pregnant?" She burst into tears and began telling me all the reasons why she couldn't have the baby. Through the inspiration of the Holy Spirit, we influenced her not to go through with her plans to abort the baby that morning. She did not. She relented, and another beautiful baby was born that same year in July. Two lives were saved by the power of prophetic prayer.

These examples demonstrate the prophetic operating by way of intercession. I wasn't aware of what my prayer would do on those days. I was praying, and God was able to use my obedience and prayers to stop the enemy's plans. Sometimes when we're praying, we aren't aware of the impact or the need, but we must pray. God had access to my life through prayer, and He intervened mightily to save lives.

So are you ready, or have you been hiding from your call? Are you afraid to give your call room to express itself? The gift and call of intercession have lives of their own. Are you like Jonah, who was angry with the people whom he was called to pray for, or have you been completely oblivious altogether? If you fit into either category, I have a way out for you. Answer the call. Give our Father your Maker, what He is expecting, asking, and seeking for—you.

CLOSING PRAYER

Father God, may I always remember the benefits of transparency and the way the truth makes me free. Your infinite wisdom always provides me with an opportunity to pray. I ask that You give me a prayer partner—someone to touch, to agree with, who provokes me to be in Your presence, who bonds with You and me, creating a threefold cord that cannot be broken and a bond that makes nothing impossible but all things possible. In Jesus's name.

CHAPTER 5

BE HEALED

Pray for one another that you may be healed. (James 5:16 NIV)

THAT YOU MAY BE HEALED

ANOTHER IMPORTANT PART OF PRAYING for one another is so that "you may be healed" or intentionally made whole. Many may see healing as only physical, but healing can be soundness of mind, reconciliation, mending, cleansing, or purifying. Our Father is intentional, and when He sets up an appointment with you, He never cancels it. His full intention is to bring every part of us into wholeness. He shows us this in 3 John 1:2, which says, "Beloved, I pray that you may prosper in all things and may be in health, even as your soul prospers" (NKJV).

Prayer has not only mended my soul but also made my body whole. Years of birth control took an adverse toll on my body. The doctor's reports were all doom and gloom. They reported an accumulation of scar tissue on my fallopian tubes, which left me semi-sterile, with only about a 20 percent chance of getting pregnant.

Isaiah 53:1 asks, "Who has believed our report? And to whom has the arm of the Lord been revealed?" (NKJV). Upon hearing the doctor's report, I thought, *Well, that's not too bad. I've already had one child and inherited a second one through my marriage, so more isn't meant to be.* I didn't think much about it until one Saturday night. I attended a church that was very sensitive to healing and deliverance. Our leaders gave Saturday nights to the Holy Spirit and fostered a presence where He could move as He willed. Saturday nights were the best services of the week, as far as I was concerned. There wasn't any preaching or teaching but only praise and adoration to the Lord, which made an opening for the Holy Spirit to do whatever He wanted—which He did. On the Saturday in question, I experienced the miraculous healing power of God for the first time. This experience wasn't secondhand or a story that someone had told me. This was my very first personal encounter with Jehovah Rophi, my Healer.

The atmosphere was electrifying. You could literally feel the presence of God as it harmoniously flowed through the building. The presence got so thick that it was penetrating. All of a sudden, I felt a surge of electricity hit my stomach. Everything in my midsection began to heat up. A sensation of heat flowed through my body, and I felt a physical shift. I felt like Jeremiah when he said, "It's like a burning fire shut up in my bones" (Jeremiah 20:9 NKJV). I fell to the floor, weeping and rolling. I left the service lighter, freer, and knowing that I was healed. I pretty much floated home. I didn't need any proof or evidence of what had happened to me that night. When God's presence touches you, there's a knowing that comes along with it and that requires no explanation. The evidence catches up with the knowing, and then you have your proof. "Heal me O Lord, and I will truly be healed; save me, and I shall be saved; for you are my Praise!" (Jeremiah 17:14 NLT)

PROPHETIC PRAYER HEALS

In less than a year, I was pregnant with my first son and our fourth child. To God be the glory. My son was born healthy, and thirteen months later, my second son was born. Two years after that, my third son entered the world. It was during my third pregnancy that the devil decided to try our faith. In my third trimester, I went in for a routine checkup. I wasn't prepared for the news that the doctor was about to give. When the doctor entered the room, I saw the file folder in his hand and his doubting face. "Looking at your sonogram, your baby has a hole opening in his back the size of a quarter." It didn't seem real. I remember him telling me not to worry because this sort of thing could be fixed once the baby was born, which was now only a few weeks away. Even with his optimism, I immediately thought, *The devil is a liar, and God's Word is true.* I was not afraid, but I was angry at the devil for taking this cheap shot at my baby. I knew the Father could heal my baby and that He was a Healer. I stood on the firm foundation of the Word and what I believed.

After receiving the news, I met my husband, filled him in on the report, and committed to standing in faith. We developed a prayer strategy and acts of faith. We anointed my stomach with oil and prophetically prayed over our unborn child. Our third son was born a few weeks later, totally healthy and whole—no signs of that devil's report. The way was easy because of wholeness by the hand of my Father. We were kept by God's power through faith in God's Word. We trusted Him and believed His Word and final say. Through these experiences, I learned that any part of our lives can change by having faith in God and speaking His Word.

God is intentionally making us whole for our calling. We must be whole in mind, heart, and emotions. The healing of the heart is so necessary for our calling. It has been extremely important that I confess and know what the Word says about me in my life. There are promises in the Word that position and sustain me in a healed place, which is important for my calling. Psalm 103:2–3 says, "Bless the Lord, O my soul, And forget not all His benefits, Who forgives all your iniquities, Who heals all your diseases" (NKJV).

God's design for my life was unfolding. Prophetic prayer was beginning to cause shifts and healing. Only through faith are all these things possible. In prayer and my relationship with the Almighty, my faith was developed.

Hebrews 11:1–3 tells us what faith is and how every kingdom was subdued, every escape was made, every affliction was conquered, and every promise was recovered. We must believe in God to pray. We must believe that He hears us and that we are having communion with Him. Without the faith that the Word of God is truth, none of this is possible. I didn't understand it all then, but today, I know that the pull of prophetic prayer was drawing me closer in relationship to and intimacy with God, which developed and grew my faith. In the transformation, the Father, Son, and Holy Spirit bring us closer to His image and likeness. We must see as He sees, hear as He hears, and do as He does. How can we answer the call if we are consumed with aliments in mind, body, or soul?

WHAT COMES OUT OF THE MOUTH

Jesus said in Matt 15:18, "But those things which proceed out of the mouth comes from the heart, and they defile a man" (NKJV). What comes out of the mouth comes straight from the heart. Jesus was clear that it was the heart that defiled and dishonored a person. If the heart is healed, the mouth will be healed. And the heart needs healing to operate in faith. My mind may be full of doubt, but I can overcome my mind if my heart can operate in faith. When the heart is wounded, condemnation can easily operate in your life. You can't be condemned and healed at the same time (see Romans 8:1 KJV). My mouth needed to be healed for me to become the mouthpiece of God. One of my favorite scriptures to pray is found in Psalm 141:3. It says, "Set a guard, O Lord, over my mouth; keep watch over the door of my lips" (AMP). This is to keep me from speaking thoughtlessly.

Do you know what you're called to do? The more radical your healing, shifting, and dealings are, the more you are called to. For example, I am called to the prophet's office, so precision, humility, love, obedience, grace, and maturity are all needed—just to name a few. This call summons special attention to the heart, mind, will, and emotions. Proverbs 4:23 says, "Keep thy heart with all diligence for out of it flows the issue of life" (KJV). Before Christ, I didn't know this scripture. The healing process is a work of sanctification for His use. The Holy Spirit sets us apart for God's use. So, the closer I became to Father God, the more healing I experienced.

> And the very God of peace sanctify you wholly and I pray God your whole spirit and soul and body be preserved blameless unto the coming of our Lord Jesus Christ. (1 Thessalonians 5:23 KJV)

He will sanctify us through and through, making us pure, whole, undamaged, consecrated to Him, and set apart for His purpose.

My help with His work is faith and belief through the Word. I must know what His Word says. What are the promises of God? And the Word says that God has redeemed me from every disease and infirmity. Whatever the Word says, that's what I say. I must take in the Word like daily supplements, and whatever the Word says, that's what I say. The Word is my anchor in faith, belief, and trust. My words can remove mountains, change lives, and create atmospheres. Therefore, I can cause my body to line up with the Word. His stripes bore my healing, giving me the power to speak forth my healing. I must know and understand that the Word has power and that it is speaking directly to me.

As a believer, we must not stress over matters that are too high for us. Devoting ourselves to prayer and making it the main thing will cause the Word to work as we give the Holy Spirit space to work in us. The strongest evidence of our love relationship with Christ is our level of personal sacrifice.

By His stripes, we are healed! (Isaiah 53:5 KJV)

God has proven His love and strength through His sacrifice. Once we are healed, we are in a position to live in His likeness, doing good and healing all who are oppressed (See Acts 10:38 KJV). God never intended for me to do this alone. His design is for me to need Him. Through prayer, I have had phenomenal reformation, which has compelled me to be healed and used by the Holy Spirit so that I may pray for others to be healed. Now that's refreshing. So what do you believe about healing? And how do you pray for others that need healing?

CLOSING PRAYER

Father God, Your Word says that you are Jehovah Rophi, the Sovereign Healer. Jesus, I call on that name whereby sickness, diseases, chains, and fears shatter. I call on that great name alone to heal my soul, set me free from infirmity, and break bondages and soul ties. I pray that every source of emotional captivity be gone, and every generational snare be annihilated. You have redeemed me from every curse of the law—poverty, sickness, and death. Let Your healing be my bread and let the living water pour over my soul to refresh, revive, and quicken me so that wholeness, health, and strength may flow through my mind, body, and soul. In Jesus's great name.

CHAPTER 6

EFFECTIVE PROPHETIC PRAYER

The effective fervent prayer of a righteous man avails much.
(James 5:16 NJKV)

EFFECTIVE RIGHTEOUSNESS

JAMES 5:16 IS A SCRIPTURE that we all know very well, but sometimes, we miss the weight of what it really means. The Amplified Version says, "The heartfelt and persistent prayer of a righteous man (believer) is able to accomplish much (when put into action and made effective by God, it is dynamic and can have tremendous power)." When we really break this scripture down, we learn that the efficient or impact-producing prayers of the righteous benefits or causes a great advantage. In other words, the prayer mentioned in James 5:16 is a productive agreement with an intended effect. It activates the power in a valid, adequate, aimed, and accomplished man or woman. He or she might display kingdom activity with strength, soundness, force, and power. This is done through extraordinary deeds. As an intercessor, it blesses me to know that God's grace equips us to be efficient and effective in prayer.

This type of prayer doesn't come without some work. We first know that it's the righteous man who bears fruit. The wonderful news is that we can't earn righteousness; it is a gift given freely. I don't have righteousness on my own. It is given to me through Christ Jesus. The scripture says that the gift of righteousness will reign in my life through Christ Jesus and that my own self-produced righteousness is like filthy rags (See Romans 5:17 NIV). Abraham, our father, believed God, and it was accounted to him as righteousness. Therefore, I cannot be what I have not believed and received in Christ. The first step in you being an effective intercessor is receiving this gift of righteousness. We start in agreement with God by faith. We are fully convinced that what He has promised, He is also able to perform. Therefore, it is accounted to us for righteousness (See Romans 4:21–22 NKJV). Developing faith and growing in it strengthens your love relationship with Him. This is necessary so that you may come into agreement with Him and have trust in your relationship together. The power of prophetic prayer is having trust and confidence in our Father, who called us to pray.

Since we know that prayer is kingdom work, productivity is necessary for the work we are putting in. Our goal is for our prayer to have an intended effect on something or someone. To have effective prayers that produce an impact, I deliberately aim what I say to the objective. I put the power or force of my whole transformed being behind what I believe, and it comes to pass. That is effective prayer.

FAITH IN GOD

Understanding how to make your prayers avail much can be difficult. But Mark 11:22–23 teaches us how. He teaches in verse 22 that we must have constant faith in God. This is where we are to begin. This is the basis of effective prayer. We must have faith in God that He is able to answer our prayers. Next in verse 23, He says, "Whoever says to this mountain," meaning that we are adequate enough to speak to a mountain. As long as we have faith, we can speak to any mountains in our lives or the lives we intercede for. Next, "You do not or cannot doubt in your heart," so you must be wholehearted and not double-minded.

Sometimes our belief in God and His ability to answer our prayers may waiver when we have hurts and wounds that are not healed. As intercessors, we must maintain a delivered heart and mind and make every effort to be made whole. Therefore, we must have faith that we are enough and that we are whole, which causes our belief to attain the power and force that are needed behind our prayers. We must know that our prayers are reaching heaven and that it is the power that is needed to drive our prayers. Then we will do extraordinary deeds, and our intended impact will be reached.

We must keep in mind that we are not effective unless we are impacted by prayer. What does this mean? It means that we are praying for people and places to properly align with God's will. We are ultimately praying for order and alignment. We speak to those things that are not, as though they were (See Romans 4:17 KJV). We elevate earthly matters, lift standards, and cause resurrection in areas of space and time. We form a relationship between the Father and earthly matters. We intercede, and as I said before, we are a bridge to connect the Father to people, places and things that have been broken down by our enemy. To do all of this, we must allow prayer to be at work in our lives personally. Do we believe that God is not a man that He should lie or the son of man that He should repent? Hasn't He said, and He will do it? Or has He spoken and not made it good? (See Numbers 23:19 NKJV). Can you trust Him? Is He dependable? Or is He like others in your life who disappoint, break promises, and abandon you? God forbids! He can, He will, He is able, and He never disappoints. This has been affirmed and verified.

EFFECTIVE FORGIVENESS

It is in the kingdom's best interest and profitable to His will that our prayers come to pass. Prayer, as described in James 5:15 (NIV), say "the prayer offered in faith will make the sick person well; the Lord will raise them up. If they have sinned, they will be forgiven" is what brings His Word and works to pass. Many miss the end of that passage of scripture. He ends it by saying that we must forgive. Otherwise, all that we've done, everything that we've prayed—even righteous, whole, powerful prayers—are all for nothing if we do not forgive. According to the dictionary's definition and the Greek word forgive means to forsake, put away, suffer, yield up, to give up all rights or claims, to grant a pardon, or to cease to feel any resentment. You cancel the debt or liability and give up the desire or power to punish completely. How can we achieve this without grace? And how do we access grace without the Spirit? Now, can we earnestly say we have *forgiven* without the Spirit, based on the definition of the word? Forgiveness is emphasized in many scriptures:

 • 1 Kings 8:39 (NIV): Hear from heaven, your dwelling place. Forgive and act;

 • 2 Chronicles 6:39 (NIV): hear prayers and supplications, maintain their cause, and forgive.

 • Psalm 86:5 (NIV): Thou, Lord, art good and ready to forgive.

 • Daniel 9:19 (NIV): Lord, hear, forgive, hearken, do, and defer not.

 • Matthew 6:12 (NIV): Forgive us our debts as we forgive.

 • Mark 2:10 (NIV): power on Earth to forgive

• 2 Corinthians 2:10 (NIV): Anyone you forgive, I also forgive.
And what I have forgiven—if there was anything to forgive—I
have forgiven in the sight of Christ for your sake

Here, we see that God hears us based on forgiveness. One could say
that He has selective hearing. He is a good Father and ready to forgive, but
He is waiting on us to forgive and to tap into the Christ in us. Our healed
heart affects others through extraordinary deeds, and forgiveness is one
of those deeds. In my own power and flesh, I don't have what it takes to
forgive, but because of James 5:15-16, I am adequate, aimed, and activated
to complete each task given, just as Christ has and continues to do.

Father God hears our prayers of forgiveness and then our prayers of
petition, supplication, declaration, etc. Our prayers of forgiveness prompt
Him to know that His ability is in us. I believe that forgiveness was
mentioned at the end of the passage because that is the key to getting our
prayers through. If we struggle with unforgiveness, we can't be righteous.
Unforgiveness makes us unrighteous, and Christ makes us righteous and
able to forgive.

In my personal journey, Father God has dealt with me twice about
forgiveness. The first time was with my mother. It was really hard for me to
believe that I harbored unforgiveness toward her. However, the Holy Spirit,
knowing all things, revealed it to me. He showed me a slideshow of events
between my mom and me when I was a teenager. I cried out to God for
months for my release and relinquishment on the hold of unforgiveness. Its
hold was so strong because I hadn't realized that it even existed. The Holy
Spirit had to reveal it to me, and that only came through prayer and alone
time with God. Finally, the Holy Spirit released me to talk to my mom.
I called her and simply said, "Mom, I forgive you for what I felt you did
wrong to me." I didn't read off a list of her crimes or reenact each scene of
pain and disappointment. I kept it simple. She even became a bit defensive
because my statement lacked a full explanation.

Nevertheless, it ended well. She accepted it, and we both moved on and became closer in heart. We had a stronger bond than we ever had before. She later accepted Christ and went home to be with Him in 2002. I still miss her, our talks and feeling her strength from her wisdom.

EFFECTIVE GRACE

Next, God dealt with me as it pertained to my husband. I've shared how great the pain was, but the deliverance was even greater. I gave my whole heart to God and constantly shut down my mind's negativity to make room for the Holy Spirit. All the emotions, inner torment, and thoughts had to be submitted to the grace that we receive as a gift. This grace is needed in our everyday lives, but most wives have no clue that it's available to us for forgiveness or how to access it. Effective prayer is allowing the Holy Spirit to pray through me according to Romans 8:26–27 (NIV). Each day, I had to give Him any connection to unforgiveness that I had toward my husband. As we pray in the Spirit, God builds and teaches us. God's love is abundantly poured out within our hearts through the Spirit (See Romans 5:5 NIV). It qualifies us as ministers of the new covenant of salvation (See 2 Corinthians 3:6 AMP). Energized by the Holy Spirit, we have a deeper understanding by the Spirit of truth (See 1 John 4:6 AMP). Finally, He gives us more and more grace to defy sin and live an obedient life (See James 4:6 AMP).

There are many more scriptures in Romans, John, Hebrews, and throughout the Bible that give us the wisdom to gain access to this grace, which breaks us free and makes a distinction in our prophetic prayers. It empowers us to become effective in everyday relationships and not only prayer. The Spirit is helping us in our weaknesses. He is making intercession for the saints and according to the will of God.

His power is made perfect in my weaknesses. His power gives me nothing but compassion, love, and submission. I had true peace, joy, and a full recovery. No longer did I have the desire to talk about past wounds and hurts. That is the grace of the Holy Spirit being expounded on. He beautifies, enhances, and embellishes humans with endowments, favor, and superior qualities such as kindness, mercy, and immunity, which can only be influenced through its origin. The Spirit of God adds moral strength to perform His Word. It causes our prayers to be effective. This effective prayer comes by allowing the Holy Spirit to pray through me according to Romans 8:26. When you are steadfast in prayer, the spirit of grace prays prophetically to break you free from bondage. That freedom makes you more effective in relationships and everyday life and not only in prayer. Freedom makes a huge difference in our lives!!

Effective Fasting

Fasting fuels our effective prayers as we learn how to fast according to scripture. One of my anchor scriptures on fasting is found in Isaiah 58:3–12. The prophet Isaiah gives us an exhaustive description of a fast that the Lord requires. Fasting is not only for food. You can fast anger, hostility, and hatred. If you desire to be effective, you must learn how to fast. A simple description of a fast is going without food, drink, or superficial soul emotions, voluntarily for religious purposes. All throughout scripture, there are examples of great leaders fasting for a day or up to forty days. They fasted on certain occasions: while opposing enemies and when faced with destructive plans, grieving, and repenting. Isaiah had the revelation of loosing the bonds of wickedness, undoing heavy burdens, feeding the hungry, sheltering the poor, and clothing the naked—in other words, sensitizing us in serving God's purposes through our fasting.

My experience with fasting has been similar to Isaiah's revelation, but it is best described in Luke 2:37 when the prophetess Anna fasted in the temple: "She served God with fasting and prayers day and night" (NKJV). This suggests that she served His purposes with her fasting and prayers. Fasting and praying together empowers us to know and serve His purposes and plans for any circumstances, situations, or seasons. It helps us to execute those purposes and plans with sensitivity and precision. We become the administrators to God's visions. Fasting afflicts the flesh and sensitizes the spirit, providing breakthrough and cooperation with the Holy Spirit as we pursue God's results.

A personal example is when I was fasting for an occasion and was oblivious to what I was about to encounter. I arrived home to find that my daughter had left home the day before and had not returned. She was completing her second year of college while living at home. With no understanding as to the reason why, I began to offer fasting with prayer. I actually came off a fast right before finding out that she was gone, but I returned to it in my distress. The next day, I went to work as usual, and within a few hours, the Holy Spirit told me to go home and pray in her bedroom. He also instructed me to pack her room up. Bewildered, I obeyed. I left work with a couple of empty boxes.

I made my way to that room. Entering it, I began to worship and praise. God's overwhelming presence came upon me. With tears in my eyes and praise on my lips, the Holy Spirit said, *Start with her bookcase. Start with this shelf. Pack it up.* The first book I pulled out revealed a drugstore pregnancy test with a positive sign on it. The Holy Spirit sweetly said, *She's afraid to face her family with the news of an unwanted pregnancy. The spirit of fear has her on the run.* I could not have that kind of precision and accuracy on my own. I was empowered. And it is available every day to us, as we yield, hear, and believe. After packing that room up and walking out with fresh knowledge and understanding, I prepared my family. We waited to hear from her, not with worry or fear but with an expectation of her return. Through the work of fasting and prayer, God's will in a distressing situation came into play and saved the day.

EFFECTIVE REPENTANCE

Repentance is another aspect of our effectiveness in prayer. Repentance requires a turning away, turning around, or changing direction to align ourselves with God properly. We must let go of disobedience, rebellion, and any sin that separates us from intimacy with God. Throughout scripture, there are examples and samples of repentance prayers and the ways that they enhance and cultivate a progressive relationship with our Savior. Let's look at David's prayer in Psalm 51:10–12, "Create in me a clean heart, O God, renew a right spirit within me" (NKJV). It covers mercy, lovingkindness, restoring, delivering, shaping, purging, and washing—all components of repentance but not an exhaustive list. The second part of turning away is bearing fruit worthy of repentance. The Holy Spirit is definitely needed through all of this. This twofold turning sets us on the straight and narrow and fast-forwards us into the kingdom that we war for and reside in.

CLOSING PRAYER

Father God, I stand on the authority of Your word—not in my own righteousness but in the righteousness of Christ Jesus. Give me a heart that desires to forgive while standing in the gap and making supplications, intercessions, and thanksgiving for all people. Holy Spirit, make my prayers effective and fervent on behalf of the kingdom so that I would be Your instrument in the earthly realm, carry out your purposes, and serve You through fasting and prayer. As I choose the fast that You have chosen, I am equipped to remove mountains, break bonds, undo heavy burdens, feed the hungry, and champion every spiritual fight. Help me, Holy Spirit, in prayer, to be ever ready with repentance and to assure my effectiveness and fervency in the Spirit. My desire is to always serve You, Father, with persistence, devotion, precision, and alertness, for such a time as this. In Jesus's mighty name.

CHAPTER 7

EARNEST PROPHETIC PRAYER

PROPHETS PRAY TOO

Elijah was a man subject to like passions as we are, and he prayed earnestly. (James 5:17 NIV)

ELIJAH THE TASKMASTER

HAVE YOU EVER BEEN TASKED to construct something? If you have children, you know the struggle. You can be faced with one hundred or more pieces and screws and a list of instructions that feel like they're in a foreign language. There are several different ways to attack the task. If you're like some people, you will read through the instructions and then organize the pieces before jumping in. The next type of person will look at the picture and take on the task without touching the instructions. The last type of person disregards the instructions and the picture and works off their intuition—and they may or may not have screws leftover and an upset child when the toy doesn't work properly.

If you're like me, you enjoy having the picture as an example and following the instructions. I use the story of Elijah similarly. He was a prophet who understood earnest prayer. His life provides an example that we, as intercessors, should follow. He personifies Proverbs 21:21: "He who earnestly seeks righteousness and loyalty finds life, righteousness and honor" (AMP). Intercession isn't a task that should be attacked without a strategy and plan, so let's take a look at Elijah's life.

Elijah, the prophet of God, was a miracle worker who lived in the northern kingdom of Israel during King Ahab's reign. He was a defender of worship and Father God. His inspirational and instructional story can be found throughout the book of 1 Kings. Elijah's purpose for arriving in Israel was to deliver God's people from Baal worship, which had been established by a wicked king who ruled Israel in that day. God sent a drought to the land at Elijah's word while he was subsequently sent to a place that was east of the Jordan, where a brook with water and ravens sustained him during the drought. When the water dried up, God sent Elijah to a widow's home for provision.

Elijah conducted his first miracle at the widow's home—the multiplication of flour and oil for food to sustain the widow, her son, and himself until the rain returned. While God sustained Elijah, Elijah sustained the widow and her son. Here, we see a powerful chain of provisions. Elijah was obedient to the instructions provided by God, he spoke at His command, and God provided adequate provision.

Elijah's second miracle was when the widow's son became ill and passed away. The Bible says that Elijah prayed and that God heard and answered him. God brought the boy back to life. At that moment, the widow knew that Elijah was a true prophet of God. Here, we see a track record of trust and obedience. Trust is the main ingredient in any love relationship and a vital instruction in the blueprint for earnest prayer. After this establishment of trust, the widow definitively knew that Elijah was a man of God. He became recognizable by walking in what he was called to do.

Next, Elijah was sent to confront the king and to challenge the god that they worshipped. Here, Elijah's trust was put to the test. Elijah prays in 1 Kings 18:36–38,

> "Lord, the God of Abraham, Isaac and Jacob. Let it be known today that you are God in Israel and that I am your servant and have done all these things at your command. Answer me, Lord answer me, so these people will know that you Lord are God, and that you are turning their hearts back again." Then the fire of the Lord fell. (NIV)

God sent down fire while his opponent said and did nothing. God demonstrated that He was the King of kings and that He alone reigned supreme. His people believed again and found faith in the living God. Rain poured, ending the drought. They were permeated with God's grace. The people of Israel turned their hearts back to God because of the prayers and obedience of Elijah.

Then Elijah told Ahab, "Go, there is the sound of heavy rain" (1 Kings 18:41 NIV). Scripture tells us that Elijah climbed to the top of Mount Carmel, bent down to the ground, and put his face between his knees. What was Elijah doing? What was going through his mind during this time? We read earlier in James 5:17, "Elijah was a man subject to like passions as we are" (NIV). How would you have felt if you were tasked with confronting the king? Would you have been afraid, unsure, or insecure? I believe that in our humanity, we trust and believe God to a certain extent, but some things seem out of reach or unattainable. I believe that those emotions may have confronted Elijah.

Instead, he trusted God at a deeper level, and when he did, God heard him. He fell on his knees in worship, extending love and prayer to the God who had called him. His track record with God was what kept him steadfast and unrelenting in his assignment. He knew his God was the provider, sustainer, healer, and miracle worker. That history with God caused his prayers to be filled with sincerity and a deep love for God. Jeremiah 33:3 says, "The word of the Lord came to him while he was still confined in the court. 'Call to me and I will answer you and tell you [and even show you] great and mighty things, [which have been confined and hidden] which you do not know, understand and cannot distinguish'" (AMP). Elijah used his earnest expectation in prayer, which was founded on his history with God. He prayed with a heartfelt effort, zeal, intent, and purpose. He took his assignment seriously, he understood that obedience to God was his highest calling, and his desire to fulfill his purpose came out in his earnest prayer. Through the depth and strength of our spiritual desire comes the intensity of our earnest, heartfelt prayers for genuine and specific assignments on the earth.

PASSION THAT CALLS GOD TO COME

Have you ever prayed not for yourself but on behalf of others who need something from God? Your earnest prayer will not provide relief until you pray and breakthrough for them. You lay down your life and sacrifice willingly, understanding that this is the greatest act of love (See 1 John 3:16 NIV).

This isn't just for those in leadership. Acts 6:4 says, "But we will give ourselves continually to prayer" (NKJV), meaning without interruption and constantly. Biblically speaking, the meaning is permanence and continuance. This is the definition of the call to earnest prayer in relationship with Father God. He is looking for someone who knows Him and has taken the time to become acquainted with His ways. It is someone who has been set apart and has carved out a place for Him in his or her life—a place where it's only about that person and Him. That individual demands His attention by offering and pledging himself or herself to something more, greater, and heavier than what he or she thinks and feels. And He answers.

When we do this, God's word comes to us. I have been taught. "Jesus doesn't come to you first; we come first." Matthew 6:33 says, "Seek ye first then all these things will be added" (KJV). I prayed earnestly and out of a place of purpose and a call to obey, and He answered me, and His word came: "Draw near to God, and He will draw near to you" (James 4:8 NKJV).

In our example from the prophet Elijah, God's words came to him. A prophet has nothing to say except God's words. What caused God's words to come? Earnest prayers do—not self-serving prayers but prayers that reach people, cities, and nations. Elijah was a human like you and me, who was subject to the same passions as we are. We all become selfishly focused on our own desires, dreams, families, and issues. But we must decide if it is worth it or not. Do we allow our passions to lead us, or do we take His passions and fulfill our purposes for living and gaining it all?

In James's writings, he tells us about our desire to have but not being able to obtain. We cannot obtain because we ask amiss, which means improperly and to consume it for our own pleasures. This is not earnest prayer. But if I walk upright before Him, He will give me the desires of my heart. Why? Because our desires become intertwined as one. This comes by way of intimacy and fellowship with our Father. Our experiences with Him deepen us and validate who He is and what He can be even to others. Then we become an example of who He is.

Elijah's experiences in prayer have helped my walk with Father God. Now I am able to share my experiences with others, which is incredible. God is still a miracle-working God who answers by fire and water. And what He did with Elijah, He can do with you or me. Where are our passions directed? Our prayers need what Elijah had: insight, foresight, and passion to pursue the impossible.

CLOSING PRAYER

Father God, show me how to be purposeful in prayer—having depth, sincere courage, and a passion for prayer. Help me to participate with You when intercession, supplications, and gap standing are needed. Make me sure and secure in Your promises and pledges that I will always pray and not faint. Let me be fully persuaded that if You said it, it shall surely come to pass, making full manifestation of Your intentions. In Jesus's name.

CHAPTER 8

MAKE IT RAIN

And he prayed again, and the heavens gave rain. (James 5:18
NKJV)

KEEP COMING

THE PROPHET ELIJAH WAS USED by God to speak a word and stay the rain.
He was used to prophesy and to show forth wonders in the heavens and
signs on the earth. However, then we read in James 5:18 that he prayed
again, and the heavens gave rain. Why did he need to pray again?

Our Father, God, does not want us to stop coming to Him. Our
worship makes Him sovereign and in charge of our wills. It sends Him a
message that we are following Him in His ordained design for our lives.
Every time we pray, a renewal happens and takes us further into His plan
and story. We are taken into a fresh experience with Him. The more we
pray, the more He knows that we trust Him. It is our responsibility to
partner with God and to receive the promise just as He gave it to Elijah. We
must trust and partner with God to make that promise manifest. When
we pray, we don't lean into our own understanding. Our understanding

and logic are limited while God's is infinite. If we pray with our own understanding and limited wisdom, we limit the miraculous in our prayer lives. Matthew 7:7–8 provides us with a formula for prayer:

Ask+keep asking=we receive.
Seek+keep seeking=we find.
Knock+keep knocking=doors will open.

Verse 8 says that everyone who keeps on asking receives and keeps seeking finds. If someone keeps on knocking, it will be opened. This scripture gives us an account of stages of answered prayer. This is a properly balanced equation for effective prayer. Answered prayer is not always done instantaneously. Taking a look further, grammatically, three vital verbs must be enacted in order for us to see manifestations. We must ask, seek, and knock. Asking means to beg, call for, crave, desire, and require. We can't stop asking or craving a thing according to His will until it is fulfilled. Asking gives me an advantage to receiving the gift and access to the hand that gives.

When I seek, I am still going after a thing, but I am looking, reasoning, striving, and demanding it. Seeking brings me in front of it so that I experience, learn, and understand it. When we seek, we are in position to recognize the arrival of the thing that we are asking for.

Finally, when we are facing a door in front of the thing we've prayed for, we knock. When we knock, we avail ourselves of what is behind the door. Knocking is an acknowledgment that we're ready for what is hidden behind the door. A simple analogy is when we order food and have it delivered to our homes. You call the restaurant and successfully place your order. As cars drive by your home, you stand in anticipation to see if the thing you've ordered has finally arrived. Before your delivery person arrives, you may be distracted by a few cars, which have come close to your home but haven't brought the thing that you're seeking. Yet you remain in position for its arrival. Finally, the doorbell rings, and you stand ready to unlock the door in total expectancy to have your hunger fulfilled. That is effective prayer. You ask, seek, and open the door to receive the thing you prayed for. Jesus said, "Here I am! I stand at the door and knock. If anyone hears my voice and opens the door, I will come in and eat with that person, and they with me." (Revelations 3:20 NIV)

Jesus is our example on every level of prayer. In Mark 8:22–25, a blind man came to Him and begged Him to touch him. So, He took the blind man by the hand and led him out of town. Jesus spit on the blind man's eyes and laid His hands on him. He asked him if he saw anything. And he looked up and said that he saw men like trees, walking. Then Jesus put His hands on his eyes again and made him look up, and he was restored. He saw everything clearly. Jesus could have spoken one word and commanded the blind man to see. But my belief is that he demonstrated the gradual and processing manifestation of answered prayers again because He was a mere man. The first prayer can set it in motion, and the second prayer gives a different result than the first prayer does.

There are many different ways to get our Father's attention. Our body is the instrument of choice. We must decide to make our body available and yielded to what glorifies our Father and brings His will to manifestation. We knock and open up to what already belongs to us as sons and daughters. Imagine someone giving us a gift that we never open. When most people receive a gift, they immediately want to know what it is. We can hardly wait, so in the car, we open it up on the way home. It is important that in our walk with Christ that we don't lose this innate characteristic. We must never fail to ask, seek, and knock. We can't give up and stop short of our blessings. Our consistency, determination, resilience, and refusal to quit will pay off. Pray and pray again, until the thing you prayed for happens.

Now there will come a time when the Holy Spirit will release you from the burden of what you are praying for. You must listen for His leading. Some may say that you are to pray once and then praise and thank Him for the answer by faith. This can be true in some areas that we pray for. However, it isn't always the case. The Bible says that Elijah prayed again, and the heavens gave rain. The first prayer was for a different result than the second was. My faith must be full in order to bring rain.

LET IT RAIN

Naturally, heat from the sun turns moisture into water vapors (gas), which disappears into the air. The vapor rises, cools, and changes into tiny water droplets, which then form clouds. When those droplets get too large and heavy, they fall as rain. This process is similar to our prayer lives. The Son heats up our prayers. Then our fired-up prayers impact the earth's atmosphere and atoms, which causes that heat (the anointing) to go into the heavens, stir up the glory, and cause the weight to infiltrate humankind. Our capacity enlarges with the water (Holy Spirit), makes it rain, and produces fruit on the earth (miracles, signs, and wonders). Rain always runs off contaminants.

Don't be afraid of the supernatural—embrace it. Television has desensitized us from the real supernatural. It should be a part of our everyday walk because we serve a supernatural God. If you read about the prophets in the Old Testament, you will see that there is always a dramatic entry in the prophetic call. Going from a prophetic intercessor to the office of a prophet explains why there were so many supernatural encounters and experiences. The prophet Elijah was a prophetic intercessor that experienced what some would call a supernatural life because of his office. The office of the prophet is different from prophesying. All can prophesy, but not all are called to the office. Praying prophetically does not mean you are called to the office of a prophet. You must discern the difference and know what you are called to do. Do not take on a heavy responsibly that you were never called to. Supernatural experiences in life are not the only indicator of the call to the office.

The prophet Isaiah put it like this in Isaiah 58:11, "And the Lord will continually guide you, and satisfy your soul in scorched and dry places. And give strength to your bones and you will be like a watered garden, like a spring of water whose waters do not fail" (NKJV). We become the spring of water that flows out into the earth and to those who are lost and in need healing, answers, or just a shift or change in their lives. I must stress the desperate need for our partnership with the Holy Spirit, who is our water source. Staying connected keeps us supplied with freshwater so that we will always be able to pour it out. Let's read Psalm 104:10–13.

> He sends the springs into the valleys …They give drink to every beast of the field, the wild donkeys quench their thirst …He waters the hills from His upper chambers, the earth is satisfied with the fruit of your works. (NKJV)

In other words, your living springs water the earth and produce fruit.

No one only takes one sip of water and is sustained for a lifetime. We must drink and give drinks throughout our lifetimes. So, when the poor and needy seek water, their tongues fail for thirst. God will not forsake them. The Lord will answer their prayers by opening rivers in desolate heights and fountains in the midst of the valleys. He will make the wilderness a pool of water and dry lands springs of water (Isaiah 41:17–18 ERV).

God promises His people that there will always be a continuous flow of water to refresh the weary, replenish the sorrowful, and satisfy the thirsty. He will find someone who is in fellowship with the Holy Spirit and fountains flowing. God can use your walk, process, cause, and deepest longing if you allow Him.

Human nature says that when we are dry and weary, we seek out water. But when you are the one with the water, the Shepard leads them to you. Job said it like this: "He speaks to the showers to the downpour of His mighty rain's" (Job 37:6 NIV). "Be Strong," and make it rain through the reign of the Holy Spirit.

Sharon Randolph

Closing Prayer

Father God, You are the substance of my prayers, which produce fruit. I am not alone. You are my God and King, who commands victories and deliverance. I'm not just asking for fruit but fruit that remains, sustains, and changes me to look more like You. My success is producing comes from Your right hand and Your arm. You and I work together. You are the source, and I am the conduit. I abide in You, and You abide in me. Our Fruit has the contents of purpose, destiny, and obedience. Help me, Father, not to waver, hesitate, or procrastinate when seeking the things that You want to produce in me for the earth. I make myself available. I keep pushing forth in prayer, faith, and belief until Your will is manifested. In Jesus's glorious name.

CHAPTER 9

SUPERNATURAL PRODUCE

And the earth brought forth her fruit. (James 5:18 NKJV)

START WITH A SEED

WHAT IS A SEED? A seed is an investment that's put into the earth for the production of something beneficial. Seeds are necessary for the germination of plants and flowers but also for our gifting. You must learn to invest in yourself—your gifting—for growth and multiplication. That investment of faith is a seed of what God can do with your abilities. It produces a working power in you, which builds, stretches, and causes you to produce. When I say spiritual production, I am referring to causes that bring forth a creative ability or supernatural power that God gives you and me.

Think about it. We can access power and produce certain results in the earth realm from the spiritual world through prayer. Communication that goes back and forth from the spiritual to the natural world causes a connection that releases fruit in abundance. Galatians 5:22–25 says, "The fruit of the Spirit is love, joy, peace, long suffering, gentleness, and self-control" (KJV). We live and walk in the Spirit. This fruit helps develop our Christlike character. This fruit is necessary if we are to overcome and crucify the works of our flesh, which only produces death.

Throughout chapter 5 of Galatians, it says that the fruit produced by the Holy Spirit supports the transformation of flesh to spirit. Since we are fleshly beings and learned first to live as flesh, we are inclined to believe that it is our primary mode of existence. But this is not true. Our natural self is spirit, and spirit rules. In verse 23 of this passage, it states, "Against such there is no law." There is no room for law or judgment in us when the fruit of the Spirit is evident in our daily lives. The Holy Spirit generates this fruit in us. We cannot manufacture this fruit on our own. It is not our responsibility alone, but we must allow the Holy Spirit to develop fruit, which becomes evident by God's power. This is not a self-help project but a decision to allow the work of the Holy Spirit in our lives.

> And the Land brought forth her fruit … land, the earth flowing
> with milk and honey. (Exodus 3:8 NIV)

God has placed fruit in the earth like a treasure, but we have to want it and seek it.

PRODUCE FRUIT

I could've missed the seasons when I learned my call and assignment. Let's be honest, we all miss some assignments from time to time. I am so grateful that I did not miss this one. My land—my treasure in the earthly realm—flows with milk and honey. It is abundant with spiritual fruit, authority in the Spirit, and a wealth of wisdom. By praying for my spouse, forgiving, and accepting my assignment, I have seen much fruit produced through the investments that I've made in my gifting.

It's similar to Ezekiel 3:1–3: "He said unto me, Son of man, eat what you find, eat this scroll and go speak to the house of Israel" (AMP). Eat what you find. Consume, feed on, and devour this appearing, attaining, acquiring, and this coming-forth occasion. Eat this scroll—the Word of God—and tell the body of Christ what you have fed on, the fruit you have borne, the vision you have acquired, and the purpose you have pursued. Without us engaging with the Spirt, destiny and purpose are unattainable. We take a chance in life, wandering aimlessly and never reaching our fullest potential. Every supernatural encounter draws us closer to discovering who we are in the spirit realm. The kingdom of God is spiritual; therefore, it is only obtained by the spirit. We may sense our call, but without true intimacy with God, we will forfeit our futures.

Let me give an excellent example of this in Matthew 21:18–22. It's a very familiar story of Jesus and His disciples returning to the city, being hungry, and seeing a fig tree by the road. When He came closer to the tree, it had leaves but no fruit. Jesus cursed the fig tree, saying, "Let no fruit grow on you ever again," and the tree withered. Why did Jesus curse the fig tree? Because it appeared to be bearing fruit by having leaves. But leaves are not fruit. Jesus is always looking for our fruit and not only our appearances and performances. Jesus finishes this story by teaching the disciples to have faith and not to doubt, all things.

Whatever you ask in prayer, believing, you will receive. Have you asked Him for any fruit lately? Help us, Father, to learn to produce fruit and not just leaves.

Just as a phone rings and we look to see who's calling, our gifting and spiritual calling should spark a similar seeking. Once I identify the call or gifting, I should then look for fruit. I caution you that this seeking can turn your life upside down—but in the most beautiful way. Some people's call will remain just that: a constant ringing in the heart with no answer. No call is complete without an answer. And our answer is only as deep as our knowledge and revelation of who we are, where we are headed, and whom we are called to influence and impact. The fullness of your realm of influence and impact is within your destiny and purpose.

In Ezekiel 3:2, the verse continues: "So I opened my mouth, and he caused me to eat the scroll" (KJV). Once I answered the call, He caused me to freely consume and attain my destiny. God said to Ezekiel, "Eat this scroll that I am giving you and fill your stomach with it." In other words, let what I am giving you consume you and fill your being. It will satisfy and propel you into your future. It is enough. Finally, Ezekiel says, "He ate it, and it was as sweet as honey in my mouth (Ezekiel 3:3 KJV)." I did eat and partake of what God prepared for me, and my prayer life produced fruit and unfolded my purpose and destiny. I have tasted the sweetness of the kingdom. It took me from the background to the forefront and from an intercessor to the office of the prophet. Questions arose in my heart, but they were no surprise to God the Father because He predestined it. This was always part of the plan. I was just oblivious to it.

The fruit of prophetic prayer in my personal walk has been so sweet. I've seen great miracles, signs, and wonders. Initially, I thought that what I was experiencing was great. Then Father God added another layer of produce. God has many layers and dimensions in store for us. Later to my surprise, God placed it on the heart of my mentor and spiritual father to ordain me in the office of prophet, in the midst of hundreds of witnesses, due to no agenda of my own. I didn't initiate it or promote it. Father God set the stage, put everyone in place, and brought it to pass. It was more than I could ever have dreamed of, imagined, or asked for. Destiny is God purposed and Holy Spirit driven. It was a predestined, inevitable course of events that brought about not only my needs and desires but also was exceedingly above and beyond all I could ever ask for.

I am convinced that in the body of Christ, we are living beneath our privileges as God's people. His way is better than anything we can ever do on our own. Unless we learn how to walk by and obey the Spirit, we will never know our Father God's limitless will. His many multidimensional purposes are nothing that the earth could ever yield on its own. John

15:4–5 says, "As the branch cannot bear fruit of itself, unless it abides in the vine, neither can you, unless you abide in Me. I Am the vine; you are the branches … without Me you can do nothing" (ESV).

When as God's mouthpiece you are chosen to edify, exhort, and comfort, you are destined to produce a special prophetic fruit in the earthly realm. This will be seen as special words of wisdom and knowledge, dreams, and visions, just to name a few. Prophetic prayer unlocks history, mysteries, and future revelations. We are living in a prophetic time, and these are the days of prophetic armies, remnants, and seasons. Ask Father God to reveal who you are and to show you if you are called to intercede, to a fivefold office, or to serve in a higher capacity. Because He is faithful, He will answer, and when He does, say yes. His grace will come and make the way easy to administrate and demonstrate the kingdom's produce on the earth. Your life will change just as mine has, and your testimony will glorify Jesus in all His splendor and glory.

When we stand to pray, let us pray this way:

> Praying always with all prayer and supplication in the Spirit, being watchful to this end with all perseverance and supplication for all the saints and for me, that utterance May be given to me, and to us, that I (we) may open my mouth boldly to make known the mystery of the gospel, for which I (we) am an ambassador in chains, that in it I may speak boldly, as I (we) ought to speak. (Ephesians 6:18–20 NKJV)

As a prophetic intercessor, my desire is to permeate the atmosphere with Spirit-led, prophetic, and prolific decrees and declarations that establish His Kingdom to come and His will to be done. Let the Word perfect our love, create our surroundings, and change our circumstances. We decree that we have the tongue of the learned and that we are able to speak a word in season to the weary, lost, and discouraged (See Isaiah 50:4 AMP). We receive instructions from His mouth and lay up His words in our hearts so that we can declare a thing, and it will be established (See Job 22:22, 28 AMP).

As Intercessors, messengers, ambassadors, believers, worshippers, and children, our words are clear, precise, aimed, and edged with authority.

> My Spirit that is upon them and My words which I shall put in your mouth shall not depart from the mouth of your true spiritual children. (Isaiah 59:21 AMP)

This is the hour where our voices must be heard. This is one of the greatest seasons of our lifetimes. The weight of His glory is in our mouths. The fire of God is upon our words, and the flame of prayer burns within our hearts. With confidence, courage, and credibility, we speak the mysteries of the kingdom.

We will not be intimidated, hesitate, or procrastinate concerning our calls. We will not allow the Holy Ghost's flow in our speech to be stifled, knowing that no weapon formed against us can prosper. We declare that the greater One abides in us. And all the enemy's strategies and plans against us falter and fail. The enemy is under our feet, and we tread upon his works, as he is powerless before us. The Word of the Lord stands firm. The Word of the Lord is pure and speaks of perfect things, to give us hope and a future of creating and cultivating life. There will be wonders in the heavens and signs on the earth. We will prophecy and call into existence things not seen, heard of, or known and declare restoration, renewal, and revival from the storehouse to the marketplace. Let the will of the Lord be done.

In Ezekiel 20:47, the Lord proclaims, "Behold, I Am about to kindle a fire in you and it will devour everyone … the blazing flame will not be quenched, and the whole surface from the South to the North will be burned, and all flesh will see that I the Lord have kindled it, and it will not be quenched" (AMP). That fire shall ever be burning upon the altar; it shall never go out (See Leviticus 6:13). Fire fall. Revival come. Consume us.

CLOSING PRAYER

Father God, thank you for your investments in me. You start new life with a seed. Take my life as a seed in your kingdom and cause me to produce spiritual fruit. Use every part of me and make me free. That I will not withhold from You. Neither would I offer you something that didn't cost me. Give me a heart of courage and the spirit of a reformer. Allow your flame to never be quenched. That I would become a fire starter. Releasing revival fires that would spread across this nation because of the fruit you are causing me to produce. I am declaring your word, wisdom and weaponry throughout the land. I am praying for strategies and strategic warfare to consume me and use me. I'm yours and you are mine for such a time as this.

CHAPTER 10

LET THE WORD DO THE WORK

> Behold, I will make my words in your mouth fire, and this
> people wood, and it shall consume them. (Jeremiah 5:14 AMP)

FIRE IN THE HOLE

HAVE YOU EVER WATCHED A boxing match where both opponents are
fighting tirelessly to overcome the other? They go through countless blows
of immense energy. Typically, we never see the rigorous training and
coaching that they endure to be adequately prepared for the match.

An intercessor goes through similar training and coaching. Every
prophetic intercessor needs a mentor to support and coach them through
life's experiences and the challenges of the journey. The Father, Son, and
Holy Spirit are in the preparation, pain, and process of the call. It is the
fight of our lives and the lives of others; however, Jesus has already won
the war, so our fight is allowing the Word to do the work and walking out
our winnings.

The prophet Jeremiah gives us a glimpse of an encounter with Israel in

Jeremiah 5:14. Through their rebellion, transgressions, and backsliding, the prophet was disrespected, and the Father was not feared. The Father's response to their arrogance was to cause His words to become fire in the mouth of the prophet and to make the people of Israel wood, so His words would consume them. The prophet who spoke His words to the nation would be filled with empowerment and authority, causing his prayers and words to ignite a flame in his being. That fire will cause our prayers to ascend quickly and consume the target. Our nation is in a similar condition, needing God's words to consume His intercessors with fire so that His words will become our words, and we will set our nation on fire.

This can be our reality if we value all scripture as God-breathed, given by divine inspiration, and being profitable for instruction, conviction of sin, correction of error, restoration to obedience, and training in righteousness. We must learn to live in conformity to God's will, both publicly and privately. We must behave honorably and with personal integrity and moral courage so that we may be complete, proficient, and thoroughly equipped for every good work (See 2 Timothy 3:16–17 AMP).

My prayer is that God consumes us with His Word so that we may be skilled in our verbiage and complete in our call. John wrote that John 3:11 that Jesus said, "We speak what we know, and testify what we have seen, but still, you people do not accept our testimony (NIV)." Therefore, the heavens will be open, angels will be at attention, and demons will flee with just one word. We must speak what we know to be true and testify of His miracles, signs, and wonders. The word of the Lord is the same word that made the heavens and all the hosts by the breath of His mouth (See Psalm 33:6). Do you remember that Matthew said that Jesus cast out the spirits with a word? The word of the Lord, which God gives, anoints, and fulfills with clarity and precision, ignites the firepower of the prophetic.

You have read many of my experiences with demons, the most

prominent ones being visitations that aggressively prohibited me from speaking. It reminds me of the text in Daniel 7:25, which says, "He (the devil), will speak words against the Most High God and wear down the saints and he will intend to change the times" (AMP). The devil knows our words are from the Spirit and that they change times, seasons, and atmospheres. His specific assignment is to silence prophetic voices. Over time, evil spirits repeated their attempts. Other leaders in the body have become discouraged and intimidated when the enemy has used people to disagree, reject, or even become angry with certain prophetic words. These tactics of our enemies are affecting our impact and effectiveness on the earth while our inspirational, God-given words lie dormant.

Nevertheless, Daniel 11:32 says, "But the people who know their God shall be strong and carry out great exploits" (NKJV). Prophetic voices must rise to the occasion. We must rise and speak out. We can no longer just talk about Jesus; we must personally know Him. Knowing Him makes us strong, and not being silent gives God access to us for great exploits. To know Him is to become spiritually mature, displaying strength and taking action. This is faith in action. This knowledge gives us mastery in the words we use. This gives us the ability to "Submit yourself to God; Resist the devil, and he will flee" (James 4:7 NKJV). No enemy can silence you without your permission. No permission can be given by those who know their God. God's Word is an indispensable weapon. In the same way, prayer is essential in this ongoing warfare. Pray hard and long. Pray for your brothers and sisters. Keep your eyes open and one another's spirits up so that no one falls behind or drops out. And do not forget to pray for me. Pray that I will know what to say and will have the courage to say it at the right time (See Ephesians 6:18–20 AMP).

The enemy is terrified of us and our capabilities in the Holy Spirit. Our words are powerful, creating, building, enlarging, and transcending. They are more powerful than we have realized. The kingdom of darkness knows that it is fighting a fight that it cannot win. But if it can convince us that we have not won, we forfeit the win. When we know that we have already won and speak that win, no matter what it looks or feels like, it does manifest. We are fighting the good fight of faith with our words. We are armed and dangerous with the right, seasoned words. Our words are an arsenal of weaponry against the works of darkness. Careless words stab like a sword, but the words of wise people bring healing (See Proverbs 12:18 GW).

Since the fall of humankind, the devil has roused us to fight against flesh and blood to take the focus off himself. He seeks to consume our thoughts, sight, and emotions with finger-pointing, faultfinding, and deception while his schemes and devices provoke us to fight against one another. He uses our words to damage and slander character, backbite, and devour one another. The arsenal that is designed for our enemies is redirected toward flesh, which profits nothing. But the Word instructs us that our weapons are not against flesh and blood but against principalities, powers, rulers, and spiritual hosts of wickedness in the darkness of this age and in the heavenly places (See Ephesians 6:12).

We should not be ignorant of the devices of the enemy. Our ignorance gives him the advantage to overtake us and causes us to perish. He sent His Word to heal and rescue us from our own destruction (See Psalm 107:20). We must make an assertive effort to come together and use our firepower of words to proclaim, decree, declare, edify, exhort, and comfort on behalf of the kingdom and against our real adversaries. We have to cause our words to unite us and divide the darkness. Let God arise and His enemies be scattered (See Psalm 68:1).

Our words have power and life. The consolation of our words can soothe the suffering, lessen the anguish, strengthen the struggling, and improve the esteem of others. We can calm seas, still storms, and change the world by our words. As we seek after God, wisdom develops our words and causes them to create like His words do. Discernment and maturity lace our words with precision, timing, and accuracy. We become His voice,

His message, and His mouthpiece. This gives us the capabilities to do greater works. Isaiah 55:11 says, "So my words that come from my mouth will not return to me empty but it will accomplish what I please and will prosper in what I send it to do" (CSB). His words are what we need to make a difference in the world. His words carry weight, influence, and power in the spirit realm.

James warned us of the power that the tongue had. It could be as deadly as poison, an unruly evil, and a world of iniquity. He continued to teach how horses had bits in their mouths to cause their bodies to obey, and ships had rudders to turn their large bodies on water. We have the Holy Spirit to tame our tongues, to bless and not curse, heal and not hurt, build up and not destroy, and make alive and not kill. The Holy Spirit is our bit and rudder. Through training, tempering, and teaching are tongues learn to speak life. We use this powerful member to restore and revive. The Lord said in Jeremiah, "Whatever I command you, you shall speak. Do not be afraid of them, for I am with you, to deliver you" (Jeremiah 1:7–9 ESV). He then proceeded to touch Jeremiah's mouth, signifying that He put His words into Jeremiah's mouth. Jesus wants to do the same thing for us. The Holy Spirit is willing and ready to aid us in speaking to our Father, our adversaries, our situations and circumstances, and one another. As David said in Psalm 34:4, "I sought the Lord on the authority of His word, He answers and delivers from all of our fears" (AMP). He is our present help in times of need.

Remember that we are like boxers but that we fight a fixed fight. His words have the greatest impact and advantage in this fight. We stand on the authority of the Word of God. When we speak and declare His words with belief, they can become fire in our mouths, which consumes everything in its path. Just as Elijah shut down the heavens from giving rain with his words, the same Spirit resides in us. But we have to yield our control to the Holy Spirit and allow Him to take over what we speak. We have been elected to see the power of God move sovereignly in the body and the world. Signs, wonders, and miracles are becoming a vital part of our everyday lives. The Word of God is a creating force. Everything around us is a product of God's Word. Psalm 33:9 says, "By the Lord's decree, the heavens were made. For He spoke, and it came into existence, He issued the decree, and it stood firm" (NET). We have an opportunity to experience His works and rehearse His wonders. Glory to God!

Paul's words to the church at Ephesus are relevant for us today.

> Now unto Him who is able to carry out His purpose, and do super abundantly more than all that we dare, ask or think (infinitely beyond our greatest prayer, hopes or dreams) according to the power that is at work within us, to Him be the glory in the church and in Christ Jesus throughout all generations forever and ever. (Ephesians 3:20 AMP)

God can carry out His purposes, but can we execute the faith and exercise the power that works within us? We can do the super things by the supernatural power that flows from the Holy Spirit when we dare to ask, think, hope, dream, and pray without limitations. With this power, we can function beyond our emotional, mental, and physical limitations. Real change and true purpose manifest in and around us and bring God glory to the nations and generations to come. Operating in this available power, through the life we live and the words we speak, presents truth, salvation, healing, deliverance, and provision. God's Word and ways are blameless and perfect.

He does not object to giving us power, but He wants to know that we can be trusted and that we are yielded and obedient to Him. He watches over His words, performs them, and makes sure they come to pass. He can't lie. If He said it, it will come to pass. We can operate in that same power, where our words come to pass as stated in Psalm 2:7–9: "I will declare the decrees of the Lord. He said to me, you are my son; this day I proclaim I have begotten you. Ask of Me, and I will assuredly give you the nations as your inheritance and the ends of the earth as your possessions" (AMP).

I can truly testify to many phenomenal experiences while praying prophetically for salvations, healings, desires, and provisions. Declaring His words back to Him or decreeing His words in the earthly realm causes changes to occur and transforms people, places, and things. Upon becoming intimately acquainted with Father God, I learned that He was looking for obedience and compassion for His people. Intimacy is a close association, detailed knowledge, or deep understanding. I caution against becoming common or accustomed with Him because when you think you have His ways down to a science, He changes His approach. His thoughts are not our thoughts, and our ways are not His ways (See Isaiah 55:8 AMP). He is always changing yet never changes. You will never have a patent on God. There are times before we call when He answers. Then at other times, we call, and He is still and in His own timing.

The most powerful times are when you think it, and it comes to pass before you even ask. You speak the words without thinking that you are praying, and they come to pass. These times are the most impacting because you realize that you are one with the Father and His Word. I would like to encourage you to keep His words in your mouth, even when you don't receive an answer. Recall the last words that He spoke to you or that you knew He was saying in your heart. Ask yourself, *Did I do what He told me to do?*

Our Father is not short of power or resources. He is not inadequate, short on delivery, or slack in His promises. If He said it, it will be. If He spoke it, it shall surely come to pass. Believe it. The Bible tells us that the secret things belong to the Lord our God but that the things which are revealed and disclosed belong to our children and us forever so that we may do all the words of this law (See Deuteronomy 29:29 NIV). It is the glory of God to conceal a matter. But the glory of kings is to search out a matter (See Proverbs 25:2 AMP). Search for it. Seek it out. Let the Word do the work. Let Him reveal the power of a son in the kingdom, who has the fire of God in his or her mouth and the flame of prayer in his or her heart. Let the Word of the Lord stand forever and ever. Let's start right now with a prophetic proclamation.

PROPHETIC INTERCESSORS PROCLAMATION

Prophetic people and intercessors, arise and let us take our places. Let's be accountable for our words—let our yes be yes and our no be no. Speak your Father's word with integrity and reverential fear. Let the words of your mouth and the meditation of your heart be acceptable and pleasing in God's sight. He is our Lord, our Rock, and our Redeemer. Lord, send your word to heal and deliver our land, bodies, and souls.

We pray, decree, and declare Your word with conviction and fortitude. Put Your words in our mouths, and we will speak to Your people all that You command. We allow Your words to be the final authority in our lives. We declare Your spoken words over our marriages, families, homes, careers, and finances. Let them permeate every aspect of our lives. We allow Your word to dwell in our hearts and minds, transforming, renewing, and making free every intricate part of our being—body, soul, and spirit.

Let the Word perfect our love, create our surroundings, and change our circumstances. We decree that we have the tongue of the learned and that we are able to speak a word in season, to the weary, lost, and discouraged. As intercessors, messengers, ambassadors, believers, worshippers, and children, our words are clear, precise, aimed, and edged with authority. The Lord says, "My Spirit which is upon you (writing the law of God on the heart), My Words which I shall put in your mouth shall not depart from the mouth, nor from the mouths of your true spiritual children" (Isaiah 59:21 AMP).

This is the hour when our voices must be heard. This is one of the greatest seasons of our lifetimes. The weight of His glory is in our mouths. The fire of God is upon our words, and the flame of prayer burns within our hearts. We speak with confidence, courage, and credibility, the mysteries of the kingdom.

We will not be intimidated, hesitate, or procrastinate concerning our call. We will not allow our speech to be stifled from the Holy Ghost's flow, knowing that no weapon formed against us can prosper. We declare that the greater One abides in us. And all the enemy's strategies and plans against us falter and fail. Our God and King decrees victories and deliverance. Through God, we push back our enemies. Through His name, we trample our enemy under our feet and tread upon his works, as he is powerless before us. The Word of the Lord stands firm.

The Word of the Lord speaks of perfect things to give us hope and a future. It creates and cultivates the fruit of the Spirit, calling into existence things not seen, heard of, or known. We declare restoration, renewal, and revival from the storehouse to the marketplace. Let the will of the Lord be done.

Ezekiel 20:47–48 proclaims, "Behold, I Am about to kindle a fire in you and it will devour everyone …The blazing flame will not be quenched and the whole surface from the South to the North will be burned by it. All flesh will see that I the Lord have kindled it, and it will not be quenched" (AMP). Fire and glory fall.

CLOSING PRAYER

Father God, You are the God who supplies the overflow, abundance, and more than enough and the all-sufficient One who gives, gives, and keeps on giving. You know my heart, capacity, and ability, even when I don't meet Your standards, I am undeserving, or I don't know how to receive Your goodness. My situation does not dictate who You are: a Miracle

Worker and the God of the impossible. Because You are a good Father, a faithful Friend, and an all-sufficient Provider, You keep me provided with grace and more grace. Through grace, all of my needs and desires are met, and they run over. Thank You for the reign of the Holy Spirit. In Jesus's name, Hallelujah!

Printed in the United States
by Baker & Taylor Publisher Services